200 *Fast*
pasta dishes

D0471680

hamlyn | **all colour cookbook**

200 *Fast*
pasta dishes

An Hachette UK Company

www.hachette.co.uk

First published in Great Britain in 2015 by Hamlyn
a division of Octopus Publishing Group Ltd, Carmelite
House, 50 Victoria Embankment, London EC4Y 0DZ

www.octopusbooks.co.uk

Copyright © Octopus Publishing Group Ltd 2015

Some of the recipes in this book have previously appeared
in other titles published by Hamlyn.

All rights reserved. No part of this work may be reproduced
or utilized in any form or by any means, electronic or
mechanical, including photocopying, recording or by any
information storage and retrieval system, without the prior
written permission of the publisher.

ISBN : 978-0-600-62901-6

A CIP catalogue record for this book is available
from the British Library.

Printed and bound in China

10 9 8 7 6 5 4 3 2 1

Both metric and imperial measurements have been
given in all recipes. Use one set of measurements only, and
not a mixture of both.

Standard level spoon measurements are used in all recipes.
1 tablespoon = 15 ml spoon
1 teaspoon = 5 ml spoon

Ovens should be preheated to the specified temperature
– if using a fan-assisted oven, follow the manufacturer's
instructions for adjusting the time and temperature.

Fresh herbs should be used unless otherwise stated.

Eggs should be medium unless otherwise stated. The
Department of Health advises that eggs should not be
consumed raw. This book contains dishes made with raw
or lightly cooked eggs. It is prudent for more vulnerable
people such as pregnant and nursing mothers, invalids, the
elderly, babies and young children to avoid uncooked or
lightly cooked dishes made with eggs. Once prepared these
dishes should be kept refrigerated and used promptly.

This book includes dishes made with nuts and nut
derivatives. It is advisable for readers with known allergic
reactions to nuts and nut derivatives and those who
may be potentially vulnerable to these allergies, such as
pregnant and nursing mothers, invalids, the elderly, babies
and children, to avoid dishes made with nuts and nut
oils. It is also prudent to check the labels of pre-prepared
ingredients for the possible inclusion of nut derivatives.

contents

introduction

This book offers a new and flexible approach to meal-planning for busy cooks and lets you choose the recipe option that best fits the time you have available. Inside you will find 200 dishes that will inspire you and motivate you to get cooking every day of the year.

All the recipes take a maximum of 30 minutes to cook. Some take as little as 20 minutes and, amazingly, many take only 10 minutes.

On every page you'll find a main recipe plus a variation, which is either quicker or a bit fancier if you have more time to spare. Whatever you choose, you'll find a huge range of super-quick recipes.

how to cook pasta

To start with, you'll need a large enough saucepan. Pasta needs a lot of water in which to cook – at least 3 litres (5½ pts) for 400 g (13 oz) pasta. Otherwise it not only won't cook evenly, but it tends to turn gummy. You will also need plenty of salt – the water should taste a little of the sea. This means adding about 1 tablespoon of salt to the pan. This will seem like a lot, but remember most of it will be drained away, leaving the pasta delicately flavoured. People often add some olive oil to the pan, but if cooked properly, this isn't really necessary.

Make sure that your water is brought to a very vigorous rolling boil over the highest heat setting before adding the pasta. Add the pasta all in one go to ensure that it cooks through uniformly. Stir with a long spoon to help prevent it from sticking, then let the water and pasta return to the boil. Leave to cook, stirring occasionally, and lowering the heat just a little if it threatens to boil over. Start timing your cooking time from the moment the pan returns to the boil. The cooking time will depend on the type of pasta and the brand. Fresh pasta cooks in a matter of minutes, while some pastas made from high-quality hard wheat take 15 minutes to cook.

how do you know it's done?

It's best to check the pasta about 2 minutes before the packet instructions suggest it will be ready. It should be al dente, which means 'to the tooth', soft and tender but with a little bite. You don't want overcooked mushy pasta that has lost all its chewy qualities. If it's underdone it will still have a chalky core and the slight taste of raw flour.

draining

Have a colander at hand when you check the pasta and when it is ready, scoop out half a mugful of water and set aside (you might need this later on when adding the sauce). Then drain the pasta straight away. Do not drain too thoroughly, though – the

hot pasta keeps cooking, which makes the water evaporate and dries it out. It should remain slippery so that it can be mixed with the sauce.

the final mixing together

Some people serve pasta and sauce separately, but to fully appreciate the flavours you need to toss them together. Tip the pasta back into the cooking pan and pour over the sauce. You want enough sauce to moisten but not drown or overwhelm the pasta. You will probably also need to add a couple of tablespoons of cooking water to the pan. Have some warmed bowls to hand and then serve straight away – remember pasta is best eaten immediately.

choosing the right pasta

People often spend more money on fresh pasta, but finding truly fresh pasta is a challenge, and making it is time-consuming, so it can be better to choose a really good-quality dry option. Italian ones are generally the best because Italian pasta manufacturers adhere to a strict set of guidelines. Choose pasta made from one-hundred percent durum wheat, this is a very hard wheat which means the pasta will maintain its shape, texture and flavour. It's this type of flour that makes pasta different from other noodles as it's so malleable and can be twisted, stretched and pressed to make hundreds of different shapes. You can also find golden egg pasta. This is silkier and smoother than plain pasta and works best with the rich butter and cream-based sauces that come from the north of Italy, while plain pasta is better with the oil-based sauces from the south.

If you are lucky enough to live near a specialist Italian shop that makes its own pasta in-house, you can buy freshly rolled sheets of pasta from them. Unlike the fresh lasagna sold pre-packaged in supermarkets, these will keep only for a day or two and are soft and malleable enough for you to make your own ravioli and tortelloni. They are also a treat, cut into small strips, used in a lasagna. For those people who are particularly health conscious there is now a wide variety of pasta shapes made from whole wheat. This darker pasta is made from wholegrain flour, which is healthier than white, refined flour but be aware that it will often take longer to cook.

In health food shops and the specialist aisles of some supermarkets you'll also see many popular pasta shapes in gluten-free form. These pastas are normally made from rice and maize flours and can be used instead of the wheat varieties, so they can be eaten by those with wheat allergies or intolerances. You can also seek out pasta coloured with vegetables and dyes – green spinach pasta is perhaps most common, but there are good varieties made from beetroot – which is purple, squash – orange and squid ink – deep black.

types of pasta

As a rule you can divide pasta into three types: filled pastas such as tortelloni, and their smaller cousins tortellini, ravioli and cannelloni tubes; long strands of pasta such as the ubiquitous spaghetti; and short tubes and shapes. What you choose depends largely on your preference (and what pasta you have in the house), but for the best results you should try to match the sauce to the pasta you are using. As a general rule, short tubes of pasta and pasta shapes are better at trapping the flavours of chunky sauces, while long strands are better paired with thinner delicate sauces.

Aside from spaghetti, which is the best-known of the strands, thicker linguine and thicker-still flat tagliatelle are also popular, as are the very thin strands called angel hair or capellini. If you want to try something different, look out for bucatini, which are thick hollow strands, or pappardelle, which are very broad ribbons of pasta.

Penne is an ever-popular pasta tube, along with the fatter rigatoni and the perennial kids' favourite, macaroni. You can also use shell-shaped pasta such as conchiglie or very large tubes such as tubetti. Other dependable shapes include farfalle, the pretty butterfly style and twists of fusilli. Artisan pastas, like uneven thick trofie and the flat discs of orcchiette, are increasingly popular, too.

how much pasta

There are no firm rules on how much pasta to cook. In Italy, pasta is normally served as part of a larger meal, while in other countries it's more often the main event. But a good rule of thumb is to allow about 100 g (3½ oz) of dried pasta per person for a main meal. The recipes in this book are easy to scale up or down for different numbers, and it's simple to add another handful to the pan if your diners look a little hungry. Also, if you wish to use a fresh pasta where dried is suggested, you will need to scale up the quantities: to make up the same finished amount, you need roughly a third more fresh pasta than you would need in dried pasta.

9

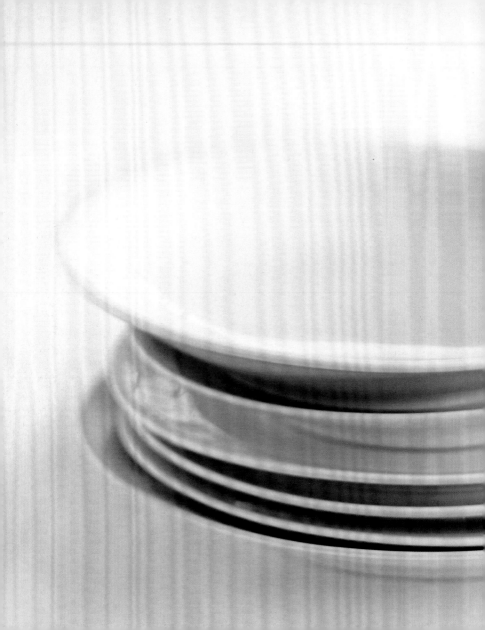

family
favourites

creamy ham & mustard pasta

Serves **4**
Total cooking time **20 minutes**

375 g (12 oz) **fusilli**
1 tablespoon **olive oil**
25 g (1 oz) **butter**
1 **onion**, thinly sliced
25 g (1 oz) **plain flour**
300 ml (½ pint) **milk**
1 tablespoon **wholegrain mustard**
1 teaspoon **Dijon mustard**
200 ml (7 fl oz) **crème fraîche**
250 g (8 oz) **smoked ham**, cut into thin strips
4 tablespoons chopped **parsley**
pepper
rocket salad, to serve (optional)

Bring a large saucepan of lightly salted water to the boil and cook the pasta for 10–12 minutes, or according to packet instructions, until just tender. Drain, return to the pan and toss with the oil.

Meanwhile, melt the butter in a large, heavy-based saucepan and cook the onion over a medium heat, stirring occasionally, for 5 minutes until softened. Add the flour and cook, stirring, for a few seconds. Remove from the heat and add the milk, a little at a time, blending well between each addition. Return to the heat, then bring to the boil, stirring constantly, cooking until thickened.

Stir in the mustards, crème fraîche, ham and parsley and heat for 1 minute more until the sauce is piping hot but not boiling. Stir in the pasta and season with pepper.

Serve in warmed serving bowls with a simple rocket salad, if liked.

For ham, mustard & tomato bake, make the recipe above, but instead of serving in warmed bowls, pour the pasta mix into a baking dish, top with 3 large, sliced beef tomatoes and sprinkle with 50 g (2 oz) grated Cheddar cheese. Cook under a preheated medium grill for 7 minutes until the tomatoes are softened and the cheese is bubbling and browned. **Total cooking time 30 minutes.**

linguine fiorentina with ham

Serves **4**
Total cooking time **20 minutes**

1 tablespoon **olive oil**
1 **onion**, finely chopped
2 **garlic cloves**, finely chopped
200 g (7 oz) **spinach leaves**,
   chopped
75 g (3 oz) **low-fat crème**
   fraîche
handful of grated **Parmesan**
   cheese, plus extra to serve
400 g (13 oz) **linguine**
100 g (3½ oz) **smoked ham**,
   sliced
salt and **pepper**

Heat the oil in a frying pan, add the onion and garlic and cook for 5 minutes until softened.

Place the spinach in a colander over the sink and pour over enough boiling water until just wilted. Squeeze out any excess water. Place in a food processor or blender with the onion and garlic, crème fraîche and Parmesan and whizz together to form a thick paste. Set aside.

Cook the pasta in a large saucepan of salted boiling water according to packet instructions until al dente. Drain, reserving a little of the cooking water, and return to the pan. Stir through the spinach mixture, adding a little cooking water to loosen.

Stir through the ham and season. Spoon into serving bowls and serve scattered with extra Parmesan.

For linguine Fiorentina ham & egg bakes, cook the recipe as above, then divide the mixture between 4 large individual soufflé dishes. Crack an egg over each one and top with a little butter. Place in a preheated oven, 180°C (350°F), Gas Mark 4, for 10 minutes or until the eggs are just cooked through. Serve immediately. **Total cooking time 30 minutes.**

tuna & sweetcorn pasta bake

Serves **4**

Total cooking time **30 minutes**

40 g (1½ oz) **butter**

40 g (1½ oz) **plain flour**

575 ml (18 fl oz) **milk**

400 g (13 oz) **fusilli**

2 x 185 g (6½ oz) **cans tuna in spring water**, drained

200 g (7 oz) **can sweetcorn**, drained

75 g (3 oz) **Cheddar cheese**, grated

25 g (1 oz) **dried white breadcrumbs**

salt and **pepper**

Melt the butter in a medium-sized saucepan and stir in the flour to make a smooth paste. Cook until golden, then gradually whisk in the milk. Bring to the boil, stirring constantly, then reduce the heat and simmer for 10 minutes until thickened, stirring occasionally. Season well.

Meanwhile, cook the pasta in a large saucepan of salted boiling water according to packet instructions until al dente. Drain and return to the pan. Mix in the white sauce, tuna, sweetcorn and the Cheddar, reserving a little for the topping.

Spoon into a medium ovenproof dish and sprinkle with the breadcrumbs and reserved cheese. Place in a preheated oven, 200°C (400°F), Gas Mark 6, for 15 minutes or until lightly browned and bubbling.

For tuna & sweetcorn pasta salad, cook 300 g (10 oz) fusilli as above. Drain, then cool under cold running water and drain again. Tip into a serving dish and stir through 6 tablespoons mayonnaise, a drained 185 g (6½ oz) can tuna in spring water and 125 g (4 oz) drained canned sweetcorn. **Total cooking time 10 minutes.**

vegetable pasta

Serves **4**

Total cooking time **20 minutes**

4 tablespoons **olive** or
   vegetable oil
2 **garlic cloves,** sliced
400 g (13 oz) **pasta shells**
   or **bows**
400 g (13 oz) **broccoli florets**
200 g (7 oz) **green beans,**
   halved
12 **cherry tomatoes,** halved
2–3 tablespoons **lemon juice**
salt and **pepper**

Warm the oil in a small pan and add the sliced garlic. Heat the pan gently for 1–2 minutes to soften the garlic and flavour the oil. Remove from the heat and set aside to infuse.

Bring a pan of lightly salted water to the boil and cook the pasta for 10–12 minutes or according to packet instructions. Add the broccoli and green beans for the final 3–4 minutes of cooking time. When the vegetables and pasta are just tender, drain well, reserving 2 tablespoons of the cooking liquid.

Stir the cherry tomatoes gently into the pasta and vegetables with the warm garlicky oil, reserved water and the lemon juice, to taste. Season with a pinch of salt and plenty of black pepper, then spoon into 4 bowls to serve.

For vegetable pasta soup, heat 2 tablespoons oil in a pan and cook 2 sliced garlic cloves gently for 1 minute. Pour in 900 ml (1½ pints) hot vegetable stock, bring to the boil, add 150 g (5 oz) vermicelli or other very small pasta shape and simmer for 2–3 minutes. Add 300 g (10 oz) broccoli florets and 2 coarsely grated courgettes. Return to the boil and simmer for 3–5 minutes until the vegetables and pasta are tender. Serve immediately with plenty of crusty bread. **Total cooking time 10 minutes.**

tomato & mascarpone penne

Serves **4**

Total cooking time **20 minutes**

500 g (1 lb) **passata**
1 **garlic clove**, crushed
2 tablespoons **olive oil**
½ teaspoon **sugar**
1 teaspoon **dried oregano**
1 teaspoon finely grated
   lemon rind (optional)
400 g (13 oz) **penne**
150 g (5 oz) **mascarpone** or
   cream cheese
salt and **pepper**

Pour the passata into a saucepan with the garlic, olive oil, sugar, oregano and lemon rind, if using. Cover loosely with a lid, bring to the boil, then simmer gently for 15 minutes.

Meanwhile, cook the pasta in a large saucepan of lightly salted boiling water for 11 minutes, or according to packet instructions, until al dente. Drain and return to the pan.

Stir the mascarpone into the pasta sauce, season lightly with salt and pepper, then pour the sauce over the pasta. Stir briefly to combine and serve immediately in shallow bowls.

For tomato & mascarpone bake, cook 350 g (11½ oz) quick-cook pasta shapes in a saucepan of lightly salted boiling water for 3 minutes, or according to packet instructions, until almost al dente. Meanwhile, combine 500 g (1 lb) passata, 1 crushed garlic clove, 2 tablespoons olive oil, ½ teaspoon sugar, 1 teaspoon dried oregano and 1 teaspoon finely grated lemon rind, if using, in a large pan, and place over a medium heat until simmering gently. Drain the pasta and stir into the sauce. Tip into a large ovenproof dish and scatter with 150 g (5 oz) grated Cheddar cheese. Cook in a preheated oven, 200°C (400°F), Gas Mark 6, for 20–25 minutes until bubbling and golden. Spoon into dishes and serve with extra cheese, if desired. **Total cooking time 30 minutes**.

spaghetti with broccoli & prawns

Serves **4**
Total cooking time **20 minutes**

400 g (13 oz) **spaghetti**
1 **small bunch of basil**, leaves
   shredded
350 g (11½ oz) **broccoli**, cut
   into small florets
2 tablespoons **olive oil**
200 g (7 oz) **cooked peeled**
   prawns
½ teaspoon **chilli flakes**
   (optional)
grated rind and juice of
   1 **lemon**
salt and **pepper**
handful of **rocket leaves,** to
   serve

Cook the spaghetti in a large saucepan of lightly salted boiling water for 11 minutes, or according to packet instructions, until al dente.

Meanwhile, cook the broccoli in a small saucepan of lightly salted boiling water for 2–3 minutes, until beginning to soften slightly, then drain.

Heat the olive oil in a small pan and warm the chilli flakes for 1 minute, if using. Add the prawns, lemon rind and juice and basil leaves, season to taste and heat through.

Drain the pasta, return to the pan and add the prawns and broccoli. Toss well to combine and heap into 4 shallow bowls. Serve topped with a few rocket leaves.

For broccoli & prawn bake, cook 300 g (10 oz) farfalle for 11 minutes, or according to packet instructions, until al dente. Meanwhile, heat 50 g (2 oz) each of butter and flour in a saucepan with 575 ml (18 fl oz) milk, stirring constantly until thickened and smooth. Simmer for 1–2 minutes to cook the flour. Cook 350 g (11½ oz) broccoli florets in lightly salted boiling water for 2–3 minutes, then drain and place in a large bowl with ½ teaspoon chilli flakes, 300 g (10 oz) cooked peeled prawns, 1 tablespoon lemon juice, and season. Stir 150 g (5 oz) crème fraîche into the white sauce and add to the bowl with the drained pasta. Stir gently to combine. Pour into a large, ovenproof dish and sprinkle with 100 g (3½ oz) fresh breadcrumbs, drizzle with 1 tablespoon oil and cook in a preheated oven, 200°C (400°F), Gas Mark 6, for 15–20 minutes until bubbling and golden. **Total cooking time 30 minutes.**

pea fusilli with bacon & ricotta

Serves **4**
Total cooking time **20 minutes**

5 tablespoons **olive oil**
2 **garlic cloves**
175 g (6 oz) **frozen peas**
handful of **mint leaves**,
    chopped, plus extra to
    garnish (optional)
squeeze of **lemon juice**, plus
    grated **lemon rind** to garnish
400 g (13 oz) **fusilli**
4 **streaky bacon rashers**
25 g (1 oz) **Parmesan**
    cheese, grated, plus extra
    to serve
100 g (3½ oz) **ricotta cheese**,
    crumbled
salt and **pepper**

Heat the oil in a small frying pan, add the garlic and cook over a very low heat for 5 minutes or until soft and golden.

Cook the peas in a small saucepan of boiling water for 2–3 minutes or until just tender. Drain, then cool under cold running water and drain again. Place half the peas, the garlicky oil, reserving a little to coat the pasta, the garlic cloves, mint, lemon juice to taste and salt and pepper in a food processor or blender and whizz together.

Cook the pasta in a large saucepan of salted boiling water according to packet instructions until al dente. Cook the bacon under a preheated medium grill for 10 minutes, turning once, or until crisp.

Drain the pasta, reserving a little of the cooking water, and return to the pan. Toss through the reserved garlicky oil, adding a little cooking water to loosen. Stir through the whole peas and Parmesan, spoon into serving bowls, top with dollops of the pea purée, the ricotta, crumble over the bacon and serve with extra mint leaves, the lemon rind and Parmesan.

For melting pea & pesto fusilli with bacon & ricotta, cook the fusilli as above. Add the full amount of peas to the pan 2–3 minutes before the end of the cooking time and cook until tender. Meanwhile, cook the bacon as above. Drain the pasta and peas, return to the pan and stir through 5 tablespoons shop-bought green pesto. Cut 125 g (4 oz) mozzarella into chunks and stir in the pasta until starting to melt. Serve, scattered with the bacon and ricotta as above. **Total cooking time 10 minutes.**

cod & leek pasta bake

Serves **4**
Total cooking time **30 minutes**

25 g (1 oz) **butter**
3 tablespoons **olive oil**
150 g (5 oz) **streaky bacon**,
  chopped
2 **leeks**, thinly sliced
350 g (11½ oz) **quick-cook
  fusilli**
500 g (1 lb) **ripe tomatoes**,
  diced
1 teaspoon finely grated
  lemon rind
2 tablespoons chopped **herbs**
  (such as parsley, chives,
  basil, rosemary or oregano)
375 g (12 oz) **skinless
  chunky cod, coley** or
  pollack fillet, cut into bite-
  sized pieces
2 tablespoons grated
  Parmesan cheese
75 g (3 oz) **fresh
  breadcrumbs**
salt and **pepper**

Melt the butter in a large, deep-sided frying pan with 1 tablespoon of the oil, and cook the bacon for 2–3 minutes, stirring occasionally, until cooked and lightly golden. Add the leeks and cook for 2–3 minutes, stirring occasionally, until softened.

Meanwhile, cook the pasta according to packet instructions, then drain and set aside.

Add the tomatoes to the bacon and leeks along with half the lemon rind and half the herbs, then season and simmer for 2–3 minutes, until the tomatoes begin to soften. Stir in the chunks of cod, then cover and simmer gently for 2–3 minutes.

Mix the Parmesan with the remaining lemon rind and herbs and the breadcrumbs, and season generously.

Stir the pasta into the tomato sauce and transfer to a large ovenproof dish. Sprinkle over the breadcrumb mixture, drizzle with the remaining oil and bake in a preheated oven, 220°C (425°F), Gas Mark 7, for 12–15 minutes, until the cod is cooked and the topping crunchy.

For cod, leek & bacon arrabbiata, heat 2 tablespoons oil in a frying pan and cook 150 g (5 oz) chopped bacon for 4–5 minutes. Add 375 g (12 oz) skinless cod, cut into chunks, and a 350 g (11½ oz) jar arrabbiata pasta sauce. Bring to the boil, reduce the heat and simmer, covered, for 3–4 minutes. Meanwhile, heat 25 g (1 oz) butter in a saucepan and cook 2 sliced leeks for 6–7 minutes. Cook 350 g (11½ oz) quick-cook fusilli according to packet instructions. Drain and divide between 4 bowls. Stir the leeks into the sauce and serve over the pasta. **Total cooking time 20 minutes.**

pesto with penne

Serves **4**
Total cooking time **20 minutes**

50 g (2 oz) **pumpkin seeds** or
  walnuts
400 g (13 oz) **wholewheat
  penne**
70 g (3 oz) **bag of rocket**
1 **small garlic clove**, crushed
50 g (2 oz) **Grana Padano
  cheese**, freshly grated
75 ml (3 fl oz) **olive** or
  vegetable oil
salt and **pepper**

Toast the pumpkin seeds or walnuts in a frying pan
over a low heat for 3–4 minutes, shaking frequently.
Tip the seeds or nuts onto a plate and set aside.

Cook the penne in a pan of lightly salted boiling water
for 11 minutes until tender, then drain.

Meanwhile, finely chop the cooled seeds or nuts in
a food processor with the rocket, garlic and cheese.
Add the oil, pouring it in a steady stream, until thick and
almost smooth. You can also make the pesto using a
pestle and mortar or chop the ingredients by hand as
finely as possible, then stir in the oil. Scrape into a bowl,
season to taste and stir into the drained pasta to serve.

For pesto pasta bake, cook 300 g (10 oz) wholewheat
penne in a pan of salted boiling water for 11 minutes
or according to packet instructions until tender. Drain.
Meanwhile, make up the pesto as above. Stir in 250 g
(8 oz) mascarpone or cream cheese and 3 diced
tomatoes. Stir the sauce into the drained pasta
and tip into a buttered ovenproof dish. Scatter over
3 tablespoons grated Grana Padano cheese, then cook
in a preheated oven, 200°C (400°F), Gas Mark 6, for
15 minutes until bubbling and golden. Serve with a
green salad. **Total cooking time 30 minutes.**

farfalle & chicken sweetcorn bites

Serves **4**

Total cooking time **20 minutes**

300 g (10 oz) **chicken mince**

2 **spring onions**, finely
   chopped

1 **egg yolk**

25 g (1 oz) **fresh white
   breadcrumbs**

50 g (2 oz) **frozen sweetcorn**,
   thawed

4 tablespoons **olive oil**, plus
   extra for greasing

400 g (13 oz) **farfalle**

3 **ready-roasted red peppers**

handful of **basil leaves**,
   chopped, plus extra to
   garnish (optional)

salt and **pepper**

Mix together the chicken, spring onions, egg yolk, breadcrumbs and sweetcorn in a bowl, then season well. Lightly wet your hands, then shape the mixture into small balls, each about the size of a walnut.

Place the chicken balls on a greased baking sheet and drizzle over 1 tablespoon of the oil. Place in a preheated oven, 200°C (400°F), Gas Mark 6, for 12–15 minutes, turning once, until cooked through.

Meanwhile, cook the pasta in a saucepan of salted boiling water according to packet instructions until al dente.

Place the red peppers, 2 tablespoons of the remaining oil and the basil in a food processor or blender and whizz together to form a chunky sauce. Drain the pasta, reserving a little of the cooking water, and return to the pan. Stir through the remaining oil and the red pepper sauce, adding a little cooking water to loosen if needed. Spoon into bowls, add the chicken bites, scatter over some basil and serve.

For chicken, sweetcorn & red pepper pasta
salad, cook 300 g (10 oz) orzo according to packet instructions, adding 100 g (3½ oz) canned sweetcorn 1 minute before the end of the cooking time. Drain, cool under cold running water and drain again. Tip into a serving dish and mix with 1 ready-cooked roasted chicken breast, skin discarded and flesh torn into shreds; 5 tablespoons mayonnaise; 1 cored, deseeded and chopped red pepper and a handful of chopped basil leaves. **Total cooking time 10 minutes.**

creamy seafood spaghetti

Serves **4**

Total cooking time **30 minutes**

15 g (½ oz) **butter**

1 **shallot**, finely chopped

100 ml (3½ fl oz) **dry vermouth**

200 ml (7 fl oz) hot **fish stock**

300 g (10 oz) **salmon fillet**

75 g (3 oz) **small cooked unpeeled prawns**

12 **scallops**, corals removed

150 ml (¼ pint) **double cream**

handful of **chives**, chopped, plus extra to garnish

400 g (13 oz) **spaghetti**

salt and **pepper**

Melt the butter in a saucepan, add the shallot and cook for 3 minutes until softened. Pour over the vermouth and bubble for 5 minutes until reduced by half. Add the stock, then place the salmon in the pan, making sure it is covered with liquid, and gently poach for 5–10 minutes or until the fish is cooked through and flakes easily. Remove from the pan, discard the skin and flake into bite-sized pieces.

Add the prawns to the pan, then add the scallops and cook for a further 2 minutes or until just cooked through. Remove the prawns and scallops and set aside with the salmon.

Add the cream to the pan and bubble until reduced down to a sauce, then season. Carefully stir in the reserved seafood, heat through and add the chives.

Meanwhile, cook the pasta in a large saucepan of salted boiling water according to packet instructions until al dente. Drain, then toss through the seafood sauce and season. Serve sprinkled with some extra chopped chives.

For simple seafood spaghetti, cook the spaghetti as above. Add 200 g (7 oz) large raw peeled prawns 3 minutes and 100 g (3½ oz) frozen peas to the pan 2–3 minutes before the end of the cooking time. Cook until the prawns turn pink and are cooked through and the peas are tender. Drain well and return to the pan, then stir through 100 g (3½ oz) crème fraîche and a handful of chopped dill. Serve at once. **Total cooking time 10 minutes.**

creamy mustard sausage pasta

Serves **4**

Total cooking time **20 minutes**

2 tablespoons **olive oil**

6 **pork sausages**

1 **onion**, thickly sliced

2 teaspoons **wholegrain mustard**

150 ml (¼ pint) hot **vegetable** or **chicken stock**

75 g (3 oz) **crème fraîche**

juice and grated rind of ½ **lemon**

400 g (13 oz) **chifferi pasta**

salt

chopped **flat leaf parsley**, to garnish

Brush a little oil over each sausage, then cook under a preheated medium grill for 15 minutes or until golden and cooked through. Cool slightly, then cut into bite-sized pieces.

Meanwhile, heat the remaining oil in a pan, add the onion and cook for 10 minutes until softened. Stir in the mustard and stock and simmer for 5 minutes, then stir in the crème fraîche and lemon juice and most of the rind.

Cook the pasta in a large saucepan of salted boiling water, according to packet instructions, until al dente while the sausages and sauce are cooking. Drain, reserving a little of the cooking water, and return to the pan. Stir through the sausages and sauce, adding a little cooking water to loosen if needed.

Spoon into serving bowls and serve sprinkled with the parsley and the remaining lemon rind.

For quick mustard & pancetta pasta, cook and drain the chifferi pasta as above. Meanwhile, heat a little olive oil in a frying pan, add 150 g (5 oz) pancetta cubes and 2 sliced garlic cloves and cook for 5 minutes. Stir in 2 teaspoons wholegrain mustard and 75 g (3 oz) crème fraîche. Stir through the drained pasta and serve as above. **Total cooking time 10 minutes.**

spicy mushroom rigatoni

300 g (10 oz) **fresh rigatoni**

2 tablespoons **olive oil**

1 **garlic clove**, finely sliced

½ **red chilli**, deseeded if liked, and chopped

150 g (5 oz) **mixed mushrooms**, preferably wild, trimmed and halved if large

grated rind of 1 **lemon**

handful of **flat leaf parsley**, chopped

salt and **pepper**

grated **Parmesan cheese**, to serve

Cook the pasta in a large saucepan of salted boiling water according to packet instructions until al dente.

Meanwhile, heat the oil in a frying pan, add the garlic, chilli and mushrooms and cook for a couple of minutes until the mushrooms colour slightly. Season well.

Drain the pasta and return to the pan. Toss through the mushroom mixture and most of the lemon rind and parsley, reserving some for garnish.

Sprinkle over the reserved lemon rind and parsley and scatter with the Parmesan and serve.

For rigatoni with baked mushrooms, place 4 trimmed field mushrooms in an ovenproof baking dish. Dot over 25 g (1 oz) butter, season well and scatter over the leaves stripped from 1 thyme sprig. Place in a preheated oven, 180°C (350°F), Gas Mark 4, for 15 minutes. Remove from the oven and chop the mushrooms. Meanwhile, cook 200 g (7 oz) dried rigatoni according to packet instructions until al dente. Drain and return to the pan, then stir through the chopped mushrooms with a squeeze of lemon juice. Serve immediately. **Total cooking time 20 minutes.**

mustard & trout pasta salad

Serves **4**

Total cooking time **20 minutes**

1 tablespoon **light olive oil**
4 **skinless, boneless trout**
  fillets, approximately
  100 g (3½ oz) each,
  seasoned lightly
400 g (13 oz) **pasta shells**
12 **cherry tomatoes**, halved
½ **cucumber**, diced

For the dressing
50 g (2 oz) **mayonnaise**
2 tablespoons **lemon juice**
3 **anchovy fillets in oil**,
  drained and roughly chopped
1 **small garlic clove**
1 teaspoon **sugar**
3 tablespoons grated
  Parmesan cheese
1 tablespoon **wholegrain**
  mustard
100 ml (3½ fl oz) **light olive** or
  groundnut oil
salt and **pepper**

Heat the oil in a nonstick frying pan and pan-fry the trout fillets for 4–5 minutes, turning once, until just cooked through but still slightly pink in the middle. Remove from the pan and set aside to cool a little.

Cook the pasta in a large saucepan of lightly salted boiling water for 11 minutes, or according to packet instructions, until al dente. Drain well, refresh under cold running water and drain again.

Meanwhile, place the dressing ingredients, except the mustard and oil, in a small food processor and blend until smooth. Transfer to a bowl and slowly whisk in the mustard and oil. Season to taste.

Flake the trout into large pieces and toss with the pasta, cherry tomatoes and cucumber. Spoon into bowls, then drizzle over the mustard dressing and serve immediately.

For trout & pasta Caesar salad, cook 400 g (13 oz) quick-cook penne according to packet instructions, cool under running water, then drain well and tip into a large bowl. Flake 250 g (8 oz) ready-cooked trout or salmon fillets into the pasta and add ½ diced cucumber, 12 halved cherry tomatoes and 8 tablespoons ready-made Caesar dressing. Mix, then spoon into 4 bowls and serve scattered with 100 g (3½ oz) ready-made croûtons, if desired. **Total cooking time 10 minutes.**

sausage spaghetti bolognese

Serves **4**

Total cooking time **20 minutes**

1 tablespoon **olive oil**

6 **garlic sausages**

1 **onion**, finely chopped

150 g (5 oz) **button mushrooms**, quartered

1 teaspoon **tomato purée**

400 g (13 oz) can **chopped tomatoes**

handful of **basil leaves**, finely chopped

125 ml (4 fl oz) **water**

400 g (13 oz) **spaghetti**

salt and **pepper**

grated **Parmesan cheese**, to serve

Heat a large frying pan until hot, then add the oil. Remove the sausages from their casings and crumble the sausagemeat into the pan. Cook for a couple of minutes, breaking up the meat with the back of a spoon. When it begins to colour, add the onion and cook for a further 5 minutes. Stir in the mushrooms and cook until they begin to soften.

Stir in the tomato purée, tomatoes, basil and measurement water. Bring to the boil, then reduce the heat and simmer for 10 minutes or until cooked through. Season well.

Meanwhile, cook the pasta in a large saucepan of salted boiling water according to packet instructions until al dente, then drain. Spoon into serving bowls and top with the sausage sauce. Serve scattered with the Parmesan.

For sausage meatball spaghetti Bolognese, remove the sausages from their casings as above and place in a bowl. Lightly wet your hands, then shape the sausagemeat into small balls. Cook in the oil as above, adding the onion, but omitting the mushrooms. Stir in 75 ml (3 fl oz) dry white wine and simmer until nearly cooked away, then add the tomato purée, tomatoes and measurement water and continue as above. **Total cooking time 30 minutes.**

broccoli & ham pasta bake

Serves **4**

Total cooking time **30 minutes**

400 g (13 oz) **spirali pasta**

125 g (4 oz) **tenderstem broccoli**, separated into florets

450 ml (¾ pint) hot **chicken or vegetable stock**

1 teaspoon **mustard**

200 g (7 oz) **crème fraîche**

150 g (5 oz) **ham**, cut into bite-sized pieces

125 g (4 oz) **Cheddar cheese**, grated

salt and **pepper**

Cook the pasta in a large saucepan of salted boiling water according to packet instructions until al dente. Add the broccoli 5 minutes before the end of the cooking time and cook until just tender. Drain and return to the pan.

Meanwhile, stir together the stock, mustard and crème fraîche in a large bowl, then mix together with the pasta, broccoli, ham and half the Cheddar. Season with salt and pepper. Spoon into an ovenproof dish and scatter over the remaining cheese.

Place in a preheated oven, 200°C (400°F), Gas Mark 6, for 15 minutes or until golden, bubbling and cooked through.

For quick broccoli & ham cavatappi, cook 500 g (1 lb) fresh cavatappi according to packet instructions until al dente, adding the broccoli as above. Meanwhile, heat a little olive oil in a frying pan, add 1 chopped garlic clove and cook for 30 seconds. Pour over 150 ml (¼ pint) passata and simmer for 5 minutes. Drain the pasta and broccoli and return to the pan. Stir through the tomato sauce and the ham as above and serve scattered with grated Parmesan cheese. **Total cooking time 10 minutes.**

chilli & anchovy dressed pasta

Serves **4**
Total cooking time **10 minutes**

400 g (13 oz) **quick-cook
  spaghetti**
3 tablespoons **olive oil**
2 **garlic cloves**, chopped
1 **red chilli**, deseeded and
  finely sliced
2 tablespoons **lemon juice**
3 tablespoons chopped **flat
  leaf parsley**
50 g (2 oz) **anchovy fillets
  in oil**, drained and roughly
  chopped
pepper

Cook the spaghetti in a large saucepan of lightly salted boiling water for 4–5 minutes, or according to packet instructions, until al dente.

Meanwhile, heat the olive oil in a small pan and add the garlic and chilli. Simmer gently in the oil for 2 minutes, until softened, then remove from the heat.

Drain the pasta and toss immediately with the garlic and chilli oil, lemon juice, parsley and chopped anchovies. Season to taste with pepper and serve in warmed bowls.

For chilli, anchovy & red pepper pasta, cut 3 red peppers in half and arrange them, cut side up, in a large roasting tin. Fill each pepper half with 2 cherry tomatoes, a little chopped garlic, 1 anchovy fillet and a scattering of chopped red chilli. Drizzle with 3 tablespoons olive oil and 2 tablespoons lemon juice, and cook in a preheated oven, 200°C (400°F), Gas Mark 6, for 20 minutes until slightly softened. Meanwhile, cook 400 g (13 oz) spaghetti in a large saucepan of lightly salted boiling water for 11 minutes, or according to packet instructions, until al dente. Tip the filled roasted peppers into a food processor, pulse briefly to make a roughly chopped sauce and toss quickly with the drained pasta. Heap into bowls and serve immediately, scattered with chopped parsley. **Total cooking time 30 minutes.**

courgette & garlic chilli fusilli

Serves **4**

Total cooking time **10 minutes**

400 g (13 oz) **quick-cook
fusilli**

300 g (10 oz) **courgettes**,
coarsely grated

4 tablespoons **olive** or
vegetable oil

1 **red chilli**, finely chopped

2 **garlic cloves**, finely chopped

2 tablespoons **lemon juice**

3 tablespoons chopped **flat
leaf parsley** (optional)

salt and **pepper**

50 g (2 oz) **Parmesan
cheese**, grated, to serve
(optional)

Cook the pasta in a large saucepan of lightly salted boiling water for 4–5 minutes, or according to packet instructions, until al dente.

Meanwhile, place the courgettes in the middle of a clean tea towel, bring up the edges and twist the courgettes in the tea towel over a sink to squeeze out the excess moisture.

Heat the oil in a nonstick frying pan with the chilli and garlic, and cook gently for 1 minute, until the oil is fragrant. Increase the heat slightly and add the courgettes. Cook gently for 5–6 minutes, until soft and golden.

Drain the pasta and stir in the courgette mixture, lemon juice and parsley, if using. Season to taste with salt and pepper, and serve immediately with the cheese, if using.

For crispy-topped courgette & garlic bake, follow the recipe above, using only 2 tablespoons parsley. Stir 250 g (8 oz) mascarpone into the pasta, season to taste and transfer to a large, ovenproof dish. Mix 75 g (3 oz) fresh breadcrumbs with 50 g (2 oz) grated Parmesan cheese and the remaining tablespoon of parsley, and sprinkle over the pasta. Cook in a preheated oven, 190°C (375°F), Gas Mark 5, for 15–20 minutes until bubbling and golden. Serve with a green salad. **Total cooking time 30 minutes.**

garlic & black pepper spaghetti

Serves **2**

Total cooking time **10 minutes**

200 g (7 oz) **quick-cook
  spaghetti**
3 tablespoons **olive oil**
2 **garlic cloves**, chopped
2 tablespoons **lemon juice**
pepper
grated **Parmesan cheese**,
  to serve

Cook the spaghetti in a large pan of lightly salted water for 3–5 minutes or according to packet instructions until just tender. Drain and return to the pan, reserving 3 tablespoons of the cooking water.

Meanwhile, heat the oil in a frying pan with the garlic and warm gently for 2–3 minutes until softened but not coloured. Pour over the cooked spaghetti with the reserved cooking liquid and lemon juice. Season with pepper. Heap into warmed bowls and serve with grated Parmesan.

For garlicky spaghetti carbonara, cook 200 g (7 oz) spaghetti in a pan of lightly salted boiling water for 10–12 minutes until tender. Meanwhile, heat 2 tablespoons oil in a frying pan and cook 150 g (5 oz) chopped bacon for 4–5 minutes over a medium heat. Add 2 chopped garlic cloves and cook for 1 minute. Set aside. Beat 1 large egg and 1 egg yolk with 4 tablespoons single or double cream, black pepper and 3 tablespoons grated hard Italian cheese. Drain the pasta and return to the pan with the bacon and the cream. Stir for a minute over a very low heat to heat and coat in the sauce. Serve with extra cheese. **Total cooking time 20 minutes.**

sausage & spinach pasta bake

Serves **4**

Total cooking time **30 minutes**

6 large pork sausages

1 tablespoon **olive oil**

500 ml (17 fl oz) **shop-bought tomato pasta sauce**

300 g (10 oz) **penne**

200 g (7 oz) **baby spinach leaves**

250 g (8 oz) **ricotta cheese**

200 g (7 oz) **mascarpone cheese**

5 tablespoons **milk**

125 g (4 oz) **mozzarella cheese**, torn

salt and **pepper**

Squeeze the sausages out of their casings into a bowl. Lightly wet your hands, then shape the sausagemeat into tiny meatballs. Heat the oil in a frying pan, add the sausage balls and cook for about 5 minutes, stirring frequently, until golden all over. Pour over the tomato pasta sauce and simmer for 5 minutes.

Meanwhile, cook the pasta in a large saucepan of salted boiling water according to packet instructions until al dente. Remove from the heat, add the spinach leaves and then drain, reserving a little of the cooking water, and return to the pan.

Mix together the ricotta, mascarpone and milk in a bowl, then stir through the pasta and season well.

Spoon the tomato and sausage sauce into a medium-sized ovenproof dish. Arrange the pasta on top and cover with the mozzarella. Place in a preheated oven, 190°C (375°F), Gas Mark 5, for 15 minutes or until golden, bubbling and cooked through.

For bacon & spinach penne, cook 4 bacon rashers under a preheated medium grill for 7 minutes or until crisp. Cool for 1 minute, then cut into small pieces. Meanwhile, cook and drain the penne and spinach as above. Toss together with the bacon and 2 chopped tomatoes. Mix 250 g (8 oz) ricotta cheese with 50 g (2 oz) feta cheese in a bowl and spoon over the pasta. Serve immediately. **Total cooking time 10 minutes.**

tomato, mussel & aubergine shells

Serves **4**

Total cooking time **20 minutes**

4 tablespoons **olive** or
   vegetable oil

2 **garlic cloves**, chopped

1 **large onion**, finely chopped

1 **red chilli**, deseeded and
   finely chopped

400 g (13 oz) **can chopped
   tomatoes**

100 ml (3½ fl oz) **water**

1 teaspoon finely grated
   lemon rind

pinch of **sugar**

400 g (13 oz) **pasta shells**

1 **aubergine**, diced

200 g (7 oz) **cooked shelled
   mussels**

Heat half the oil in a saucepan, add the chopped garlic, onion and chilli, and cook for 1–2 minutes, until just softened. Add the tomatoes, measured water, lemon rind and sugar, then season to taste and simmer gently for 15–18 minutes.

Cook the pasta shells in a large saucepan of lightly salted boiling water for 11 minutes, or according to packet instructions, until al dente.

Meanwhile, heat the remaining oil in a large frying pan and cook the aubergine for about 8 minutes, turning occasionally, until golden. Transfer to the simmering pan of tomato sauce for the remaining cooking time.

Stir the mussels into the tomato sauce for the final minute, cook until thoroughly heated through, then spoon over the drained pasta to serve.

For tomato & mussel fusilli, cook 400 g (13 oz) quick-cook fusilli according to packet instructions. Heat 4 tablespoons olive or vegetable oil in a pan, add 2 chopped garlic cloves and 1 deseeded and finely chopped red chilli, and cook for 1–2 minutes. Add 300 g (10 oz) defrosted frozen mussels, cook for 1 minute, then stir in 4 diced tomatoes, 1 teaspoon finely grated lemon rind and 1 tablespoon lemon juice. Season generously to taste, then toss immediately with the drained pasta and spoon into bowls to serve. **Total cooking time 10 minutes.**

grilled cheese & bacon tortellini

Serves **4**

Total cooking time **20 minutes**

800 g (1 lb 10 oz) **fresh
    tortellini**, such as tomato-
    and-basil filled

 2 tablespoons **olive oil**

200 g (7 oz) **bacon**, diced

150 g (5 oz) **mushrooms**,
    sliced (optional)

400 g (13 oz) **half-fat crème
    fraîche**

75 g (3 oz) **blue cheese**,
    such as Stilton or Roquefort,
    crumbled

black pepper

100 g (3½ oz) **Cheddar
    cheese**, grated

green salad, to serve
    (optional)

Cook the pasta in a large pan of lightly salted boiling
water for 2–3 minutes, or according to packet
instructions, until tender. Drain, reserving 3 tablespoons
of the cooking water, then tip the tortellini into 1 large
or 4 individual ovenproof dishes.

Meanwhile, heat the oil in a frying pan and cook
the bacon over a medium heat for 4–5 minutes, until
browned. Add the mushrooms and cook for a further
3–4 minutes, until golden.

Stir in the crème fraîche and reserved cooking water,
the blue cheese and a pinch of black pepper. Heat
gently until the cheese has melted, then pour the
mixture over the pasta.

Sprinkle with the Cheddar and slide the dish(es) under
a preheated medium-hot grill for 6–7 minutes, or until
bubbling and golden. Serve with a green salad, if liked.

For cheesy penne with crispy bacon, grill 8 streaky
bacon rashers under a preheated medium-hot grill for
6–7 minutes. Cook 700 g (1 lb 7 oz) fresh penne in a
pan of salted boiling water for 2–3 minutes. Drain and
return to the pan with 2 tablespoons of the cooking
water. Meanwhile, melt 25 g (1 oz) butter in a frying pan
and cook 150 g (5 oz) mushrooms for 3–4 minutes.
Stir in the crème fraîche, blue cheese and black pepper
from the main recipe. When the cheese has melted, stir
the mixture into the pasta. Crumble the crispy bacon
over the top and serve immediately. **Total cooking time
10 minutes.**

mushroom & tarragon rigatoni

Serves **4**

Total cooking time **20 minutes**

50 g (2 oz) **butter**

1 tablespoon **olive** or **vegetable oil**

1 **large leek**, thinly sliced

1 **garlic clove**, chopped

150 g (5 oz) **mushrooms**, sliced

1 teaspoon **dried tarragon**

400 g (13 oz) **rigatoni** or **tortiglioni**

100 ml (3½ fl oz) **dry white wine** or **vegetable stock**

250 ml (8 fl oz) **single cream**

salt and **pepper**

4 teaspoons grated **Parmesan cheese**, to serve

Heat the butter and oil in a large nonstick frying pan until the butter is frothing. Add the leek and garlic, and cook for 2–3 minutes, until beginning to soften. Add the mushrooms and tarragon, and cook for a further 4–5 minutes, until soft and golden.

Meanwhile, cook the pasta in a large saucepan of lightly salted boiling water for 11 minutes, or according to packet instructions, until al dente.

Pour the white wine and cream into the mushrooms, and season generously with salt and pepper. Simmer gently for 6–7 minutes.

Drain the pasta and stir into the sauce. Spoon into 4 bowls and serve immediately, sprinkled with grated Parmesan.

For quick creamy mushroom penne, heat 50 g (2 oz) butter and 1 tablespoon oil in a large frying pan. Add 1 thinly sliced large leek and 1 chopped garlic clove, and cook for 2–3 minutes. Add 150 g (5 oz) sliced mushrooms and 1 tablespoon chopped fresh tarragon, and cook for a further 4–5 minutes. Meanwhile, cook 400 g (13 oz) quick-cook penne pasta according to packet instructions. Stir 150 g (5 oz) cream cheese and 8 sliced sun-dried tomatoes into the mushrooms with 250 ml (8 fl oz) single cream, then bring to the boil and season. Pour over the drained pasta and serve with 4 teaspoons grated Parmesan cheese. **Total cooking time 10 minutes.**

spaghetti & prawn tomato sauce

Serves **4**

Total cooking time **10 minutes**

500 g (1 lb) **fresh spaghetti**
2 tablespoons **olive oil**
2 **garlic cloves**, sliced
2 x 400 g (13 oz) **cans
    chopped tomatoes**
3 tablespoons **sun-dried
    tomato paste**
250 g (8 oz) **large cooked
    peeled prawns**
25 g (1 oz) **basil**, roughly
    chopped
salt and **pepper**
freshly grated **Parmesan
    cheese**, to serve (optional)

Bring a large saucepan of lightly salted water to the boil and cook the spaghetti for 3 minutes, or according to packet instructions, until al dente, then drain.

Meanwhile, heat the oil in a large, heavy-based frying pan and cook the garlic over a medium heat for a few seconds to flavour the oil, then add the tomatoes and tomato paste and cook, stirring occasionally, for 5 minutes until thickened.

Add the prawns and basil, stir through and heat through for 1–2 minutes until the prawns are piping hot. Season generously with pepper, then add the drained pasta and toss with the sauce to mix.

Serve in warmed serving bowls, sprinkled with freshly grated Parmesan cheese, if liked.

For prawn, tomato & garlic bake, cook 500 g (1 lb) fresh penne according to packet instructions, then drain. Meanwhile, heat 2 tablespoons olive oil in a large pan and cook 2 sliced garlic cloves over a medium heat, stirring, for 2 minutes. Add 6 tablespoons sun-dried tomato paste and 2 x 400 g (13 oz) cans chopped tomatoes. Bring to the boil, then simmer, uncovered, for 10 minutes until the sauce has reduced by a quarter. Add 250 g (8 oz) large cooked, peeled prawns, 4 tablespoons chopped basil, then toss the pasta into the sauce. Transfer to a gratin dish and scatter over 100 g (3½ oz) grated Gruyère cheese. Cook under a preheated high grill for 5 minutes until golden. **Total cooking time 30 minutes.**

pork & mushroom tagliatelle

Serves **4**
Total cooking time **20 minutes**

400 g (13 oz) **tagliatelle**
2 tablespoons **olive** or
    vegetable oil
300 g (10 oz) **pork fillet**, cut
    into thin strips
300 g (10 oz) **field
    mushrooms**, sliced
1 **lemon**, sliced, to garnish
100 ml (3½ fl oz) **dry white
    wine**
1 teaspoon **dried tarragon**
200 ml (7 fl oz) **double cream**
salt and **pepper**

Cook the tagliatelle in a large saucepan of lightly salted boiling water for 8 minutes, or according to packet instructions, until al dente.

Meanwhile, heat the oil in a deep-sided frying pan and fry the pork strips for 6–7 minutes, until golden. Remove with a slotted spoon and set aside in a bowl.

Add the mushrooms to the pan and cook for 3–4 minutes, until soft and golden. Remove and add to the pork.

Arrange the lemon slices in a single layer in the pan and cook for 2–3 minutes, turning once, until golden. Remove and set aside.

Pour the wine and tarragon into the pan, and bubble to reduce by half. Return the mushroom and pork to the pan and pour in the cream. Season well. Simmer gently for 2–3 minutes, until thickened slightly, then serve immediately alongside the tagliatelle, garnished with the lemon slices.

For bacon & mushroom tagliatelle, cook 400 g (13 oz) quick-cook tagliatelle according to packet instructions. Meanwhile, heat 2 tablespoons oil in a frying pan and cook 200 g (7 oz) chopped thick-cut bacon for 3–4 minutes. Add 300 g (10 oz) sliced field mushrooms and cook for 3–4 minutes. Stir in 2 teaspoons chopped fresh tarragon and 275 ml (9 fl oz) single cream, then season and bring to the boil. Stir in 1 tablespoon lemon juice and serve with the tagliatelle. **Total cooking time 10 minutes.**

rich tomato & chilli spaghetti

Serves **4**

Total cooking time **20 minutes**

250 g (8 oz) **spaghetti**
2 tablespoons **olive oil**
2 **shallots**, finely chopped
1 **red chilli**, finely chopped
2 **garlic cloves**, thinly sliced
500 g (1 lb) **tomatoes**,
  roughly chopped
3 tablespoons **sun-dried
  tomato paste**
150 ml (¼ pint) **red wine**
6 tablespoons chopped
  parsley
salt and **pepper**
freshly grated **Parmesan
  cheese**, to serve (optional)

Bring a large saucepan of lightly salted water to the boil and cook the spaghetti for 8–10 minutes, or according to packet instructions, until al dente. Drain, return to the pan and toss with 1 tablespoon of the oil.

Meanwhile, heat the remaining oil in a large, heavy-based frying pan and cook the shallots, chilli and garlic over a medium heat, stirring frequently, for 2–3 minutes until slightly softened. Add the tomatoes, increase the heat and cook, stirring occasionally, for 5 minutes until beginning to soften. Stir in the tomato paste and wine, cover and simmer for 10 minutes until thick and pulpy.

Stir in the parsley and season with pepper. Add the cooked spaghetti and toss well to coat in the sauce. Serve with freshly grated Parmesan, if liked.

For easy tomato, chilli & black olive spaghetti, bring a large saucepan of salted water to the boil and cook 250 g (8 oz) quick-cook spaghetti for 8–10 minutes, or according to packet instructions, until al dente. Drain, return to the pan and toss with 1 tablespoon olive oil. Meanwhile, heat 2 tablespoons olive oil in a large frying pan and cook 2 finely chopped shallots, 1 finely chopped red chilli and 2 thinly sliced garlic cloves over a medium heat, stirring, for 2–3 minutes until softened. Add a 500 g (1 lb) jar red-wine-flavoured ragu sauce and a drained 250 g (8 oz) jar pitted black olives, chopped, and heat through. Stir in 6 tablespoons chopped parsley, season with pepper and serve with freshly grated Parmesan cheese. **Total cooking time 10 minutes.**

minestrone with pasta & beans

Serves **4**

Total cooking time **30 minutes**

2 tablespoons **olive oil**

1 **onion**, chopped

1 **celery stick**, chopped

1 **carrot**, chopped

1 **garlic clove**, crushed

400 g (13 oz) **can chopped tomatoes**

1.5 litres (2½ pints) **vegetable stock**

1 **rosemary sprig**

150 g (5 oz) **small soup pasta**

75 g (3 oz) **cavolo nero** or **other cabbage**, shredded

200 g (7 oz) **canned cannellini beans**, rinsed and drained

4 tablespoons **fresh green pesto**

25 g (1 oz) **Parmesan cheese**, grated

salt and **pepper**

crusty bread, to serve

Heat the oil in a large, heavy-based saucepan. Add the onion, celery and carrot and cook for 5 minutes until softened, then add the garlic and cook for a further 1 minute. Pour in the tomatoes and stock, add the rosemary and bring to the boil. Reduce the heat and simmer for 15 minutes.

Add the pasta and cabbage and cook for 5–7 minutes, or according to packet instructions. Stir in the beans and heat through, then season to taste. Ladle the soup into warmed bowls, drizzle with the pesto, sprinkle with the Parmesan and serve with crusty bread.

For spring vegetable minestrone with beans, heat 1 tablespoon olive oil in a large, heavy-based saucepan. Add 1 chopped onion and cook for 5 minutes until softened. Stir in 1 crushed garlic clove and cook for 30 seconds. Pour in 1.5 litres (2½ pints) hot vegetable stock and the rind of ½ lemon, pared in wide strips, and simmer for 5 minutes. Remove the strips of lemon rind and add 200 g (7 oz) canned cannellini beans, rinsed and drained, 1 finely chopped courgette and 150 g (5 oz) peas or French beans. Simmer for 3–5 minutes until the vegetables are just tender, then stir in a handful of chopped basil and serve with crusty bread. **Total cooking time 20 minutes.**

macaroni cheese with bacon

Serves **4**

Total cooking time **20 minutes**

300 g (10 oz) **macaroni**

2 tablespoons **olive** or **vegetable oil**

150 g (5 oz) **smoked streaky bacon**, chopped

100 g (3½ oz) **mushrooms**, sliced or chopped

500 ml (17 fl oz) **milk**

50 g (2 oz) **plain flour**

50 g (2 oz) **butter**

150 g (5 oz) **medium** or **mature Cheddar cheese**, grated

pinch of **ground nutmeg** (optional)

freshly ground black pepper

Cook the macaroni in a large saucepan of lightly salted boiling water for 8–10 minutes, or according to packet instructions, until al dente.

Meanwhile, heat the oil in a frying pan and cook the bacon for 3–4 minutes, until cooked and lightly golden. Add the mushrooms and cook for a further 3–4 minutes, until softened. Remove from the heat and set aside.

Pour the milk into a saucepan with the flour and butter, and cook over a medium heat, whisking constantly, until thickened and simmering gently. Cook for 2–3 minutes, then remove from the heat and stir in half the grated cheese.

Drain the pasta and combine with the cheese sauce, bacon and mushrooms. Add the nutmeg, if using, and season with black pepper. Tip into a large ovenproof dish, scatter over the remaining cheese and cook under a preheated grill for 5–6 minutes, until golden and bubbling. Serve immediately.

For cheesy mushroom & ham macaroni, cook 400 g (13 oz) quick-cook macaroni according to packet instructions. Meanwhile, heat 2 tablespoons oil in a deep-sided frying pan and cook 100 g (3½ oz) sliced mushrooms for 3–4 minutes, until softened. Add 275 ml (9 fl oz) double cream, 150 g (5 oz) chopped ham, 150 g (5 oz) grated medium or mature Cheddar cheese, a pinch of ground nutmeg and seasoning, and heat until bubbling gently. Drain the pasta, stir into the sauce and serve immediately. **Total cooking time 10 minutes.**

ham & courgette lasagne

Serves **4**

Total cooking time **30 minutes**

500 ml (17 fl oz) **ready-made tomato pasta sauce**

6 **slices of ham**, cut into bite-sized pieces

handful of **basil leaves**, chopped

1 **courgette**, grated

8 **fresh lasagne sheets**

150 ml (¼ pint) **crème fraîche**

6 tablespoons **water**

25 g (1 oz) **Parmesan cheese**, grated

salt and **pepper**

Place the tomato pasta sauce in a saucepan and heat through, then stir in the ham, basil and courgette and season to taste.

Meanwhile, prepare the lasagne sheets according to packet instructions. Mix together the crème fraîche and measurement water in a bowl until smooth.

Spread a third of the tomato sauce over the bottom of a medium-sized ovenproof dish. Drizzle a quarter of the crème fraîche over the sauce, then top with a third of the lasagne sheets, cutting to fit the dish, if necessary. Repeat with the remaining ingredients, finishing with the remaining crème fraîche, and scatter with the Parmesan.

Place in a preheated oven, 200°C (400°F), Gas Mark 6, for 15 minutes or until bubbling and cooked through.

For Parma ham & courgette open lasagne, cook 8 fresh lasagne sheets in a large saucepan of salted boiling water for 3–5 minutes or until soft, then drain well and cut into squares. Meanwhile, heat the grated courgette and basil in the tomato pasta sauce as above, adding 4 slices of chopped Parma ham. Pile up the lasagne squares on a plate, layering with the tomato sauce. Serve topped with a dollop of crème fraîche. **Total cooking time 10 minutes.**

healthy
feasts

lemon & broccoli pasta salad

Serves **4**

Total cooking time **20 minutes**

375 g (12 oz) **penne** or
  rigatoni
150 g (5 oz) **broccoli florets**
100 g (3½ oz) **frozen
  edamame beans**
100 g (3½ oz) **frozen peas**
100 g (3½ oz) **sugarsnap
  peas**, trimmed
150 g (5 oz) **soft cheese with
  garlic and herbs**
finely grated zest and juice of
  1 lemon
4 tablespoons **olive oil**
1 **red chilli**, deseeded and
  finely chopped
100 g (3½ oz) **grated
  pecorino cheese**
2 tablespoons chopped
  tarragon leaves
salt and **pepper**

Cook the pasta in a large saucepan following the
packet instructions, adding the broccoli florets,
edamame beans, peas and sugarsnaps for the final
3 minutes of its cooking time.

Drain the pasta and vegetables, saving a ladleful of
the cooking water, then tip back into the pan.

Stir in the soft cheese, lemon zest and juice, olive oil,
chilli, pecorino, tarragon, some seasoning and a splash
of cooking water.

Serve the salad warm or at room temperature.

For broccoli, pasta & mixed pea bake, tip 500 g
(1 lb) cooked rigatoni into a greased ovenproof
dish with 150 g (5 oz) blanched broccoli florets,
100 g (3½ oz) peas, 100 g (3½ oz) soya beans and
100 g (3½ oz) blanched sugarsnap peas. Toss to mix
well. In a separate bowl whisk together 3 eggs with
1 tablespoon finely grated lemon zest, 2 tablespoons
finely chopped tarragon, 1 chopped red chilli and 150 g
(5 oz) soft cheese with garlic and herbs. Season well.
Pour the egg mixture into the ovenproof dish, sprinkle
over 100 g (3½ oz) grated pecorino cheese and bake
in a preheated oven, 220°C (425°F), Gas Mark 7,
for 15–20 minutes or until the mixture is bubbling
and lightly golden on the top. Serve hot or at room
temperature. **Total cooking time 30 minutes.**

spicy fish soup

Serves **4**
Total cooking time **20 minutes**

2 tablespoons **olive oil**
1 **garlic clove**, sliced
1 **red chilli**, deseeded
and finely chopped, plus
extra sliced chilli to serve
(optional)
½ teaspoon **ground cumin**
1 teaspoon **paprika**
1.5 litres (2½ pints) hot **fish
stock**
400 g (13 oz) **white fish**, such
as cod or haddock, skinned,
boned and cut into bite-sized
chunks
150 g (5 oz) **stelline pasta**
juice of ½ **lemon**
salt and **pepper**
fresh coriander sprigs,
to garnish

Heat the oil in a large saucepan, add the garlic and chilli
and cook for 30 seconds until beginning to turn golden.
Stir in the cumin and paprika, then pour over the stock.

Bring to the boil, then reduce the heat, season, add the
fish and simmer for 5 minutes.

Add the pasta and cook for a further 7–10 minutes
until the fish and pasta are cooked through.

Ladle into serving bowls and drizzle over the lemon
juice to taste. Serve with sprigs of fresh coriander, and
sliced chilli, if liked.

For tomato & spicy prawn soup, place 300 ml
(½ pint) shop-bought tomato pasta sauce and 750 ml
(1¼ pints) hot fish stock in a saucepan and bring to
the boil. Add the chilli, spices and stelline pasta as
above, then simmer for about 7 minutes until the pasta
is cooked through. Add 150 g (5 oz) cooked peeled
prawns to the pan 2 minutes before the end of the
cooking time and cook until they are heated through.
Serve immediately. **Total cooking time 10 minutes.**

crunchy parma ham pappardelle

Serves **4**
Total cooking time **30 minutes**

75 ml (3 fl oz) **olive oil**, plus
   extra to serve
6 **sage leaves**
rind of ½ **lemon**, cut into strips
100 g (3½ oz) **shop-bought
   cooked and peeled
   chestnuts**, halved if liked
400 g (13 oz) **pappardelle**
juice of ½ **lemon**
50 g (2 oz) **rocket leaves**
150 g (5 oz) **Parma ham**
salt and **pepper**

Place the oil in a medium-sized pan, add the sage leaves and lemon rind and heat very gently for about 10 minutes. Add the chestnuts and cook gently for a further 10 minutes. Remove from the heat and set aside for 10 minutes.

Meanwhile, cook the pasta in a large saucepan of salted boiling water according to packet instructions until al dente. Drain.

Remove the lemon rind and sage leaves from the oil. Toss together the chestnut lemon oil with the pasta.

Pile on to serving plates and arrange the rocket and Parma ham on top. Serve immediately with a squeeze of lemon juice over each portion.

For simple Parma ham & chestnut pappardelle,

cook and drain the pappardelle as above. Meanwhile, heat a little olive oil in a frying pan, add the Parma ham and cook until sizzling. Remove from the pan and add the chestnuts, prepared as above, and 1 sliced garlic clove. Cook for a further 3 minutes until golden. Squeeze over the juice and grated rind of 1 lemon, then toss through the drained pasta with the Parma ham, broken into small pieces. Serve sprinkled with chopped flat leaf parsley. **Total cooking time 10 minutes.**

tuna & aubergine arrabiata

Serves **4**
Total cooking time **20 minutes**

1 tablespoon **olive oil**
1 **onion**, finely chopped
2 **garlic cloves**, finely chopped
1 **aubergine**, diced
650 g (1 lb 7 oz) **passata**
100 ml (3½ fl oz) **red wine**
½–1 teaspoon **chilli flakes**
75 g (3 oz) **pitted green
  olives with hot chilli
  peppers** or **chilli-stuffed
  olives**, sliced
1 **small bunch of basil**, leaves
  stripped
pinch of **sugar**
400 g (13 oz) **penne**
2 x 185 g (6½ oz) **cans tuna
  chunks in spring water**,
  drained
finely grated **Parmesan
  cheese**, to serve (optional)
salt and **pepper**

Heat the oil in a large, deep-sided frying pan over a medium heat, add the onion and garlic and cook for 4–5 minutes, stirring occasionally, until softened and lightly golden.

Bring two pans of lightly salted water to the boil. Add the aubergine to one saucepan and cook for 3–4 minutes until almost tender, then tip into a colander and drain well.

Meanwhile, pour the passata and red wine into the pan with the onions, add the chilli flakes, olives, basil and sugar and season with salt and pepper. Add the well-drained aubergines and bring to the boil, then reduce the heat and simmer gently for 12–15 minutes until thickened slightly.

Cook the pasta in the second pan of boiling water, while the sauce is simmering, for 11 minutes, or according to packet instructions until al dente.

Drain the pasta, stir the tuna into the sauce, add the pasta and serve with a little Parmesan sprinkled over, if liked.

For quick pasta with aubergine & tomato sauce, cook 500 g (1 lb) fresh penne in salted boiling water according to packet instructions. Meanwhile, roughly chop 6 ripe tomatoes and 200 g (7 oz) grilled aubergines or mixed antipasti and fry over a medium heat. Add 75 g (3 oz) sliced chilli-stuffed olives, chopped leaves from 1 small bunch of basil, 1 deseeded and finely chopped red chilli and stir. Drain the pasta, add the tomato mixture to the pasta and stir to combine. Serve. **Total cooking time 10 minutes.**

dill-dressed salmon pasta salad

Serves **4**
Total cooking time **10 minutes**

350 g (11½ oz) **fresh fusilli**
2 **spring onions**, sliced
¼ **cucumber**, chopped
150 g (5 oz) **smoked salmon**,
    cut into strips

For the dill dressing
75 g (3 oz) **crème fraîche**
4 tablespoons **mayonnaise**
handful of **dill**, finely chopped
salt and **pepper**

Cook the pasta in a large saucepan of salted boiling water according to packet instructions until al dente. Drain the pasta, then cool under cold running water and drain again.

Meanwhile, to make the dill dressing, mix together the crème fraîche, mayonnaise and dill in a bowl and season with salt and pepper.

Tip the pasta into a serving dish and stir through the spring onions, cucumber, smoked salmon and dill dressing.

For summery poached salmon & dill pasta, cut 1 fennel bulb into slices and place in a saucepan with a 400 g (13 oz) piece of salmon fillet. Pour over 100 ml (3½ fl oz) dry white wine, enough fish stock to cover and a couple of dill sprigs. Bring to the boil and then simmer for 10–12 minutes until the fish is cooked through and flakes easily. Remove the fish and fennel with a slotted spoon. Flake the fish into large chunks, removing any skin and bones, and keep warm with the fennel. Boil the poaching liquid until reduced down to 75 ml (3 fl oz), then stir through 3 tablespoons crème fraîche. Meanwhile, cook and drain the fresh fusilli as above. Stir through the sauce, fennel and salmon. Sprinkle with a little chopped dill and serve immediately. **Total cooking time 20 minutes.**

fusilli amatriciana with pancetta

Serves **4**
Total cooking time **30 minutes**

2 tablespoons **olive oil**
1 **red chilli**, deseeded if liked,
and finely chopped
250 g (8 oz) **pancetta slices**,
cut into strips
1 **onion**, finely chopped
1 **rosemary sprig**, leaves
stripped and chopped
100 ml (3½ fl oz) **fruity red
wine**
400 g (13 oz) **can chopped
tomatoes**
200 ml (7 fl oz) **water**
400 g (13 oz) **fusilli**
salt and **pepper**
grated **Parmesan cheese**, to
serve

Heat a frying pan until hot, add the oil, chilli and
pancetta and cook until beginning to crisp. Add the
onion and rosemary and cook for a further 3–5 minutes
until lightly coloured.

Pour over the wine and bubble until reduced by half,
then add the tomatoes and the measurement water and
leave to simmer for at least 20 minutes until thickened.
Season well.

Meanwhile, cook the pasta in a large saucepan of
salted boiling water according to packet instructions
until al dente. Drain and return to the pan, then toss
through the sauce.

Spoon into serving bowls and serve scattered with the
Parmesan cheese.

For bacon & sun-dried tomato fusilli, heat a little
butter in a frying pan, add 1 trimmed, cleaned and
sliced leek and cook for 5 minutes until beginning to
soften. Cut 4 bacon rashers into small strips, add to the
pan with 2 sliced spring onions and cook for a further
5 minutes. Pour over 25 ml (1 fl oz) dry white wine and
cook for 3 minutes until reduced. Stir in 3 drained and
chopped sun-dried tomatoes in oil and 4 tablespoons
crème fraîche. Meanwhile, cook and drain the fusilli
as above, then toss through the sauce. Serve at once.
Total cooking time 20 minutes.

tuna & white bean pasta

Serves **4**

Total cooking time **20 minutes**

75 ml (3 fl oz) **single cream**

400 g (13 oz) **can cannellini
beans**, rinsed and drained

225 g (7½ oz) **can tuna in oil**,
drained

325 g (11 oz) **ferretto pasta**

salt and **pepper**

For the gremolata

1 **garlic clove**

grated rind of 1 **lemon**

handful of **flat leaf parsley**,
chopped

Place the cream and beans in a saucepan and cook
for 15 minutes or until the beans are very soft, adding
a little water if needed. Stir the tuna into the sauce.

Meanwhile, cook the pasta in a large saucepan of
salted boiling water according to packet instructions
until al dente.

Make the gremolata. Place the garlic, lemon rind and
parsley on a board and chop until fine but not mushy.

Drain the pasta, reserving a little of the cooking water.
Mix together the pasta and tuna sauce, adding a little
cooking water to loosen if needed.

Spoon into serving bowls and serve scattered with
the gremolata.

For quick tuna & white bean penne, cook 400 g
(13 oz) fresh penne according to packet instructions
until al dente. Add the cannellini beans as above
to the pasta pan 2 minutes before the end of the
cooking time. Drain and return to the pan. Stir through
2 tablespoons crème fraîche, the grated rind of 1
lemon, the tuna as above and a handful of chopped
flat leaf parsley. Serve immediately. **Total cooking
time 10 minutes.**

pasta with salmon & capers

Serves **4**

Total cooking time **20 minutes**

400 g (13 oz) **casareccia pasta**
100 ml (3½ fl oz) **dry white wine**
150 ml (¼ pint) **double cream**
250 g (8 oz) **smoked salmon**, cut into strips
75 g (3 oz) **rocket leaves**
½ **red onion**, thinly sliced
grated rind of ½ **lemon**
2 teaspoons **capers**, drained
salt and **pepper**

Cook the pasta in a large saucepan of salted boiling water according to packet instructions until al dente.

Meanwhile, heat the wine in a saucepan until boiling, then reduce the heat and simmer for 5 minutes. Stir through the cream, season and leave to bubble for a couple of minutes.

Drain the pasta, reserving a little of the cooking water, and return to the pan. Stir through the sauce, adding a little cooking water to loosen if needed. Toss through the remaining ingredients and serve immediately.

For salmon, red onion & rocket pasta salad, cook 300 g (10 oz) orzo according to packet instructions. Drain, then cool under cold running water and drain again. Meanwhile, mix together 2 tablespoons natural yogurt, 4 tablespoons mayonnaise and plenty of black pepper in a bowl. Tip the pasta into a serving dish and stir through the yogurt with the smoked salmon, rocket, onion, lemon rind and capers as above. **Total cooking time 10 minutes.**

broccoli & chilli orecchiette

Serves **4**

Total cooking time **20 minutes**

350 g (11½ oz) **broccoli**, cut
into florets

300 g (10 oz) **orecchiette**

4 tablespoons **olive oil**

3 **shallots**, diced

4 **garlic cloves**, finely chopped

1 teaspoon **dried chilli flakes**

2 tablespoons chopped
parsley

2 tablespoons **Parmesan
cheese** shavings, to serve

Steam the broccoli for 4–5 minutes, until just tender
and drain.

Cook the orecchiette in a saucepan of boiling water
for 11–13 minutes, or according to packet instructions,
until al dente.

Meanwhile, heat 2 tablespoons of the olive oil in a
frying pan and sauté the shallots with the garlic and
chilli flakes for 3–4 minutes.

Add the broccoli to the frying pan and stir to coat with
the spicy oil.

Drain the pasta and add to the frying pan with the
remaining oil and chopped parsley. Toss together well.

Serve sprinkled with Parmesan shavings.

For broccoli & tuna pasta bake, cook 200 g (7 oz)
fresh penne in a saucepan of boiling water according
to the packet instructions, until al dente. Meanwhile,
steam 300 g (10 oz) broccoli florets for 4–5 minutes
until just tender. Drain the penne and broccoli and mix
together in an ovenproof dish with 4 chopped tomatoes
and a drained 400 g (13 oz) can tuna. Pour over 350 ml
(12 fl oz) warmed ready-made cheese sauce and
sprinkle with 4 tablespoons fresh breadcrumbs and
2 tablespoons grated Parmesan cheese. Place under
a preheated hot grill for 3–4 minutes until golden.
Serve with a crisp green salad. **Total cooking time
10 minutes.**

pasta niçoise

Serves **4**

Total cooking time **10 minutes**

400 g (13 oz) **ditalini pasta**

150 g (5 oz) **green beans**,
   trimmed

200 g (7 oz) **can tuna in
   spring water**, drained and
   flaked

100 g (3½ oz) **cherry
   tomatoes**, quartered

50 g (2 oz) **pitted black olives**
   (preferably Niçoise)

75 g (3 oz) **rocket leaves**

salt

For the dressing

3 **anchovy fillets in oil**,
   drained and chopped

1 **garlic clove**, crushed

2 teaspoons **white wine
   vinegar**

2 tablespoons **extra virgin
   olive oil**

Cook the pasta in a large saucepan of salted boiling water according to packet instructions until al dente. Add the beans 5 minutes before the end of the cooking time and cook until just tender.

Meanwhile, make the dressing. Mash together the anchovies and garlic in a bowl, then mix in the vinegar and oil.

Drain the pasta and beans, reserving a little of the cooking water, and return to the pan. Stir through the dressing, adding a little cooking water to loosen if needed. Mix through the remaining ingredients and serve immediately.

For pasta Niçoise with griddled fiery tuna, make the recipe as above, omitting the canned tuna. Meanwhile, rub 1 tablespoon olive oil and a pinch of dried chilli flakes over 4 tuna steaks and season well. Heat a griddle pan until smoking, add the tuna steaks and cook for 3–5 minutes on each side, until browned on the outside but still rare inside. Slice the griddled tuna and add to the pasta. **Total cooking time 20 minutes.**

rigatoni with a fresh tomato sauce

Serves **4**
Total cooking time **30 minutes**

6 **large ripe plum tomatoes**
1 tablespoon **extra virgin
    olive oil**
2 **garlic cloves**, finely diced
1 **red chilli**, deseeded and
    finely diced
75 ml (3 fl oz) **vegetable
    stock**
25 g (1 oz) **basil leaves**, finely
    chopped
375 g (12 oz) **rigatoni**
grated **Parmesan cheese**, to
    serve (optional)
salt and **pepper**

Place the tomatoes in a bowl and pour over boiling
water to cover. Leave for 1–2 minutes, then drain,
cut across the stem end of each tomato, and peel off
the skins.

Cut the tomatoes in half horizontally, when cool enough
to handle, and shake or gently spoon out the seeds
then finely dice the flesh.

Heat the oil in a large, nonstick frying pan and add the
garlic and chilli. Cook on a medium-low heat for 1–2
minutes or until the garlic is fragrant but not browned.

Add the tomatoes, stock and basil, season well and cook
gently for 6–8 minutes or until thickened, stirring often.

Meanwhile, cook the rigatoni according to packet
instructions until al dente, drain and toss into the
tomato sauce mixture.

Spoon into warmed bowls and serve with grated
Parmesan, if desired.

For tomato, chilli & mozzarella pasta bake, preheat
the oven to 220°C (425°F), Gas Mark 7. Place
500 g (1 lb) cooked rigatoni in a shallow ovenproof
dish and spoon over 2 x 350 g (11½ oz) tubs of fresh
ready-made tomato and basil sauce. Season, add a
finely chopped red chilli, toss to mix well and then top
with 400 g (13 oz) sliced mozzarella cheese. Bake for
15–20 minutes or until golden and bubbling. Serve
immediately. **Total cooking time 20 minutes.**

quick beef bolognese

Serves **4**

Total cooking time **20 minutes**

1 **onion**, roughly chopped

1 **carrot**, roughly chopped

1 **celery stick**, trimmed and roughly chopped

1 **large field mushroom**, about 100 g (3½ oz), roughly chopped

1 tablespoon **olive oil**

2 **garlic cloves**, finely chopped

350 g (11½ oz) **lean beef mince**

400 g (13 oz) **spaghetti**

300 g (10 oz) **fresh ready-made tomato pasta sauce**

300 ml (½ pint) **boiling water**

½ teaspoon finely grated **lemon** rind

½ teaspoon **dried oregano**

4 teaspoons grated **Parmesan cheese**, to serve (optional)

salt and **pepper**

Put the onion, carrots, celery and mushroom in a food processor or blender and pulse until finely chopped.

Heat the olive oil in a large, deep-sided frying pan over medium heat, tip in the chopped vegetables and cook for 3 minutes, stirring occasionally. Add the garlic and cook for 2–3 minutes until softened, stirring frequently. Tip in the mince, increase the heat to high and cook for 2–3 minutes until browned.

Meanwhile, bring a large saucepan of lightly salted water to the boil and cook the spaghetti for 11 minutes, or according to packet instructions, until al dente.

Pour the tomato sauce for pasta into the pan with the meat with the measured boiling water, lemon rind and oregano. Season with salt and pepper, reduce the heat, cover loosely and simmer for about 10 minutes, or until thickened.

Drain the pasta and serve in bowls topped with the bolognese sauce and a little grated Parmesan, if liked.

For penne Bolognese bake, cook 300 g (10 oz) penne in lightly salted boiling water for about 10 minutes until al dente, or according to packet instructions. Make the quick beef bolognese as above, then stir into the drained pasta. Scrape into an ovenproof dish, sprinkle over 2 tablespoons grated Parmesan cheese and place in a preheated oven, 230°C (450°F), Gas Mark 8, for 8–10 minutes until bubbling. **Total cooking time 30 minutes.**

turkey meatball & pasta soup

Serves **4**

Total cooking time **30 minutes**

500 g (1 lb) **turkey mince**
50 g (2 oz) **fresh white
  breadcrumbs**
25 g (1 oz) **Parmesan
  cheese**, grated, plus extra
  to serve (optional)
2 tablespoons finely chopped
  flat leaf parsley, plus extra
  to garnish
1 **egg**, lightly beaten
1 **garlic clove**, crushed
2.5 litres (4 pints) hot **chicken
  stock**
2 **large carrots**, peeled and
  thinly sliced
175 g (6 oz) **farfalline pasta**
salt and **pepper**

Mix together the turkey, breadcrumbs, Parmesan, parsley, egg and garlic in a large bowl and season to taste. Lightly wet your hands, then shape the mixture into small balls about 2 cm (¾ inch) round.

Bring the stock to the boil in a large saucepan, then add the carrots and simmer for 5 minutes.

Drop the turkey meatballs into the stock and cook for 5 minutes. Add the pasta and cook for a further 5–7 minutes or until the meatballs are cooked through. Season to taste.

Ladle into bowls and serve sprinkled with a little Parmesan and chopped parsley, if liked.

For simple turkey soup, bring 1 litre (1¾ pints) hot chicken stock to the boil, then add 2 peeled and grated carrots and cook for 3 minutes. Stir in the pasta as above and cook for 5–7 minutes or until cooked through, adding 200 g (7 oz) shredded cooked turkey slices 1 minute before the end of the cooking time to heat through. Serve sprinkled with finely chopped dill. **Total cooking time 10 minutes.**

spicy smoked salmon pasta

Serves **4**

Total cooking time **20 minutes**

400 g (13 oz) **bucatini,**
   linguine or **spaghetti**
200 g (7 oz) **asparagus tips**,
   halved lengthways
1 tablespoon **butter**
1 tablespoon **olive oil**
1 **red chilli**, finely chopped
1 teaspoon **dried red chilli**
   flakes
2 **garlic cloves**, finely chopped
2 **shallots**, finely chopped
200 g (7 oz) **crème fraîche**
200 g (7 oz) **smoked salmon**,
   roughly chopped
100 g (3½ oz) **frozen peas**
4 tablespoons finely chopped
   dill
salt and **pepper**

Cook the pasta in a large saucepan of lightly salted boiling water according to packet instructions until al dente, adding the asparagus 2 minutes before the end of the cooking time.

Heat the butter and oil in a large frying pan, add the red chilli, chilli flakes, garlic and shallots and cook over a medium heat for 2–3 minutes.

Drain the pasta and asparagus, then add to the frying pan with the crème fraiche, smoked salmon, peas and chopped dill and heat through until piping hot, then season.

Serve in warm bowls with a crisp green salad.

For spicy smoked salmon pasta salad, cook 200 g (10 oz) fresh penne, 100 g (3½ oz) frozen peas and 400 g (12 oz) asparagus tips in a pan of lightly salted boiling water for 2–4 minutes, or according to the pasta packet instructions, until the pasta is al dente. Drain, refresh under cold running water and drain again. Put in a salad bowl with 400 g (12 oz) chopped smoked salmon. Mix together 1 teaspoon dried red chilli flakes, 1 teaspoon medium curry powder and 175 ml (6 fl oz) shop-bought French salad dressing. Pour over the pasta, toss and serve. **Total cooking time 10 minutes.**

pea & spring onion linguine

Serves **4**

Total cooking time **20 minutes**

6 tablespoons **olive oil**

2 **garlic cloves**, chopped

a large handful of **mint leaves**

50 g (2 oz) **toasted pine nuts**

50 g (2 oz) **Parmesan cheese**, grated

350 g (11½ oz) **linguine**

225 g (7½ oz) **fresh** or **frozen peas**

4 **spring onions**, sliced

Place the olive oil, garlic, mint, pine nuts and grated Parmesan in a blender or food processor and blend until smooth.

Cook the linguini in a saucepan of boiling water according to packet instructions, until al dente.

Meanwhile, cook the peas in a saucepan of boiling water for 3–4 minutes and then drain.

Drain the pasta. Return to the pan and gently stir in the mint pesto, peas and spring onions. Serve immediately.

For spaghetti with pea & mint pesto, cook 400 g (13 oz) quick-cook spaghetti for 3–5 minutes, or according to packet instructions, until al dente. Meanwhile, blanch 250 g (8 oz) frozen peas in a saucepan of boiling water for 2 minutes, then drain and refresh under cold water. Place the peas in a food processor with 2 crushed garlic cloves, 50 g (2 oz) toasted pine nuts, 50 g (2 oz) grated Parmesan cheese, 6 tablespoons extra virgin olive oil, a small handful of mint leaves and some salt and pepper. Pulse briefly until roughly chopped, but not smooth. Drain the spaghetti, then return to the pan with the pesto and toss together well. Serve sprinkled with Parmesan cheese shavings. **Total cooking time 10 minutes.**

roasted vegetable pasta

Serves **4**

Total cooking time **30 minutes**

1 **red pepper**, deseeded and chopped

1 **yellow pepper**, deseeded and chopped

1 **red onion**, cut into wedges

2 **courgettes**, sliced

2 **carrots**, peeled and sliced

2 **garlic cloves**, sliced

8 **baby tomatoes**

2 tablespoons **olive oil**

2 teaspoons **cumin seeds**

275 g (9 oz) **penne**

75 g (3 oz) **pitted black olives**

2 tablespoons **pesto sauce**

small handful of **basil leaves**, torn

salt and **pepper**

Parmesan cheese shavings, to serve

Place all the vegetables, garlic and tomatoes in a large roasting tin and sprinkle with the oil, cumin seeds and some salt and pepper. Roast in a preheated oven, 200°C (400°F), Gas Mark 6, for 26–28 minutes.

Bring a large pan of water to the boil, halfway through the cooking time, and cook the pasta for 9–12 minutes, or according to packet instructions, until al dente.

Drain the pasta and toss in the roasted vegetables, olives, pesto sauce and basil leaves.

Serve sprinkled with Parmesan shavings.

For pasta & green vegetable salad, cook 350 g (11½ oz) penne in boiling water for 8–9 minutes. Meanwhile, in another pan of boiling water, blanch 125 g (4 oz) sugarsnap peas, 125 g (4 oz) trimmed green beans and 125 g (4 oz) peas for 3 minutes. Drain and refresh under cold running water. Drain the pasta, then toss with the vegetables, 2 tablespoons pesto sauce, 150 g (5 oz) crumbled feta, 25 g (1 oz) rocket leaves and 2 tablespoons toasted pine nuts. **Total cooking time 10 minutes.**

spaghetti with mini tuna balls

Serves **4**

Total cooking time **20 minutes**

2 **spring onions**, thinly sliced
2 x 185 g (6½ oz) **cans tuna
in spring water**, drained
1 **egg yolk**, lightly beaten
50 g (2 oz) **fresh white
breadcrumbs**
handful of **mint leaves**,
chopped, plus extra to
garnish (optional)
pinch of **dried chilli flakes**
1 tablespoon **olive oil**
375 ml (13 fl oz) **shop-bought
tomato pasta sauce**
400 g (13 oz) **spaghetti**
salt and **pepper**

Mix together the spring onions, tuna, egg yolk, bread-crumbs, mint and chilli flakes in a bowl and season. Lightly wet your hands, then shape the mixture into small balls, each about the size of a walnut. The mixture should make about 12 balls.

Heat the oil in a nonstick frying pan and cook the tuna balls for 5–10 minutes or until golden all over and cooked through. Pour over the tomato pasta sauce and cook for a further 5 minutes until the sauce is heated through, adding a little extra water if the sauce becomes too thick.

Meanwhile, cook the pasta in a large saucepan of salted boiling water according to packet instructions until al dente. Drain and stir through the sauce.

Spoon into serving bowls and serve sprinkled with extra chopped mint, if liked.

For spaghetti with spiced fresh tuna balls, chop a 400g (13 oz) piece of fresh tuna on a chopping board as finely as you can. Make the mini tuna balls as above, replacing the canned tuna with the fresh tuna and adding 1 teaspoon ground cumin and 15 g (½ oz) raisins. Continue with the recipe as above. **Total cooking time 30 minutes.**

chicken, tomato & feta pasta

Serves **4**

Total cooking time **20 minutes**

2 tablespoons **olive oil**

2 **boneless, skinless chicken breasts**

1 teaspoon **honey**

juice of 1 **lemon**

200 g (7 oz) **cherry tomatoes**

400 g (13 oz) **rotelle pasta**

handful of **oregano leaves**, chopped

25 g (1 oz) **feta cheese**

salt and **pepper**

Brush a little of the oil over each chicken breast, then place on a baking sheet and season well. Place in a preheated oven, 200°C (400°F), Gas Mark 6, for 12 minutes or until nearly cooked through.

Drizzle over the honey and a good squeeze of the lemon juice and scatter the tomatoes around. Return to the oven and cook for a further 5 minutes or until the chicken is cooked through.

Meanwhile, cook the pasta in a large saucepan of salted boiling water according to packet instructions until al dente. Drain, reserving a little of the cooking water, and return to the pan. Stir through more lemon juice to taste, the remaining oil and the oregano.

Cut the chicken into bite-sized pieces and stir through the pasta with the tomatoes, adding a little cooking water if needed. Spoon into serving bowls, crumble over the feta cheese and serve immediately.

For simple chicken, tomato & feta tagliatelle, cook and drain 400 g (13 oz) tagliarelle according to the packet instructions until al dente. Toss through 2 ready-cooked roasted chicken breasts, skin discarded and flesh torn into shreds, a large handful of drained sun-blush tomatoes in oil and a little balsamic vinegar to taste. Serve sprinkled with basil leaves and the feta as above. **Total cooking time 10 minutes.**

chickpea & tomato linguine

Serves **4**
Total cooking time **20 minutes**

2 tablespoons **olive oil**
1 **onion**, chopped
2 **garlic cloves**, crushed
1 **celery stick**, sliced
400 g (13 oz) **can chopped tomatoes**
175 g (6 oz) **baby spinach leaves**
400 g (13 oz) **can chickpeas**, rinsed and drained
350 g (11½ oz) **linguine**
10 **basil leaves**, torn
50 g (2 oz) **Parmesan cheese**, grated, to serve

Heat the oil in a large saucepan, add the onion, garlic and celery and cook for 3–4 minutes until softened. Add the tomatoes and bring to the boil, then reduce the heat and simmer for 10 minutes. Stir in the spinach and chickpeas and cook until the spinach is wilted.

Meanwhile, cook the pasta in a saucepan of boiling water for 6–8 minutes, or according to packet instructions, until al dente. Drain, then add to the tomato sauce with the basil and toss together.

Serve sprinkled with the Parmesan.

For chickpea, tomato & pasta salad, cook 300 g (10 oz) farfalle in a saucepan of boiling water for 7–8 minutes, or according to packet instructions, until al dente. Drain, then refresh under cold running water and drain again. Place in a serving bowl and toss together with a rinsed and drained 400 g (13 oz) can chickpeas, 1 diced red onion, 4 chopped tomatoes, 6 torn basil leaves, 50 g (2 oz) rocket leaves, 2 tablespoons Parmesan cheese shavings, 2 tablespoons olive oil and 1 tablespoon balsamic vinegar. Season to taste and serve. **Total cooking time 10 minutes.**

seafood & butternut pasta

Serves **4**

Total cooking time **30 minutes**

400 g (13 oz) **butternut squash**, peeled, deseeded and cubed

2 tablespoons **olive oil**

400 g (13 oz) **tripoline pasta**

1 **onion**, finely chopped

2 **garlic cloves**, finely chopped

1 **red chilli**, deseeded if liked, and finely chopped

75 ml (3 fl oz) **dry white wine**

500 g (1 lb) **mussels**, debearded and cleaned

salt and **pepper**

chopped **fresh coriander leaves**, to garnish

Toss the butternut squash in 1 tablespoon of the oil in a roasting tin and season well. Place in a preheated oven, 200°C (400°F), Gas Mark 6, for 15 minutes. Turn over and cook for a further 10 minutes or until soft and lightly browned.

Meanwhile, cook the pasta in a large saucepan of salted boiling water according to packet instructions until al dente.

Heat the remaining oil in another large saucepan, add the onion, garlic and chilli and cook for a couple of minutes until softened. Pour over the wine and bring to the boil. Reduce the heat and simmer for 1–2 minutes. Add the mussels, cover with a lid and cook for 5 minutes until the mussels have opened. Discard any that remain closed.

Drain the pasta and return to the pan. Stir in the butternut squash and mussels with all the cooking juices. Season well.

Spoon into serving bowls and serve sprinkled with the fresh coriander.

For easy butternut squash & seafood tripoline, cook 400 g (13 oz) tripoline and the butternut squash, prepared as above, in a large saucepan of boiling water for 10 minutes until soft. Drain, return to the pan and toss together with 200 g (7 oz) shop-bought ready-cooked mussels, a good squeeze of lemon juice and some dried chilli flakes. Serve as above. **Total cooking time 10 minutes**.

salmon, tomato & chilli pasta

Serves **4**

Total cooking time **20 minutes**

2 tablespoons **olive oil**
250 g (8 oz) **piece of salmon fillet**
1 **onion**, finely chopped
2 **garlic cloves**, finely chopped
1 teaspoon **tomato purée**
1–2 tablespoons **sweet chilli sauce**
400 g (13 oz) **can chopped tomatoes**
400 g (13 oz) **pasta shells**
salt and **pepper**
basil leaves, to garnish

Rub 1 tablespoon of the olive oil over the salmon and season well. Place on a baking sheet and cook in a preheated oven, 190°C (375°F), Gas Mark 5, for 12–15 minutes or until the fish is cooked through and flakes easily.

Meanwhile, heat the remaining oil in a saucepan, add the onion and garlic and cook for a couple of minutes until softened. Stir in the tomato purée, then add the sweet chilli sauce and tomatoes. Bring to the boil, then reduce the heat and simmer until ready to serve.

Cook the pasta in a large saucepan of salted boiling water according to packet instructions until al dente. Drain, reserving a little of the cooking water, and return to the pan. Stir through the tomato sauce, adding a little cooking water if needed. Carefully flake the fish, removing any skin and bones, and add to the pasta.

Spoon into serving bowls and serve sprinkled with basil leaves.

For quick gnocchi with chilli tomatoes & salmon, cook and drain the gnocchi according to packet instructions. Meanwhile, mix together 200 g (7 oz) halved cherry tomatoes, 3 tablespoons sweet chilli sauce and a handful of chopped basil leaves in a bowl. Stir into the drained pasta with 2 hot-smoked salmon fillets torn into bite-sized pieces. Serve immediately. **Total cooking time 10 minutes.**

spicy pesto linguine

Serves **4**

Total cooking time **20 minutes**

200 g (7 oz) **potatoes**, peeled and cut into small cubes

200 g (7 oz) **green beans**, trimmed and halved

350 g (11½ oz) **linguine**

2 **red chillies**, finely chopped

250 g (8 oz) **shop-bought fresh green pesto**

salt and **pepper**

grated **pecorino cheese**, to serve

Cook the potatoes in a large saucepan of lightly salted boiling water for 10–12 minutes or until just tender, adding the beans 4 minutes before the end of the cooking time. Drain well, then return to the pan.

Meanwhile, cook the pasta in a separate saucepan of boiling water according to packet instructions until al dente, then drain and add to the potatoes and beans.

Mix together the red chillies and pesto in a bowl, then season well. Spoon into the pasta mixture and toss to mix well.

Spoon into warm bowls and serve with grated pecorino cheese to sprinkle over.

For spicy green bean & pesto pasta gratin, cook 250 g (11½ oz) dried penne in a large saucepan of lightly salted boiling water according to packet instructions until al dente, adding 400 g (12 oz) trimmed and chopped green beans 2 minutes before the end of the cooking time. Meanwhile, mix together 2 finely chopped red chillies, 250 g (8 oz) shop-bought fresh green pesto, 200 g (7 oz) mascarpone cheese and 2 lightly beaten eggs. Drain the pasta and beans, then put in a lightly greased shallow ovenproof dish. Pour over the pesto mixture and toss to mix well. Sprinkle over 100 g (3½ oz) dried breadcrumbs and place in a preheated oven, 200°C (400°F), Gas Mark 6, for 10–15 minutes or until piping hot. Serve with a rocket salad. **Total cooking time 30 minutes.**

crab & mussel tagliatelle

Serves **4**

Total cooking time **20 minutes**

2 tablespoons **olive oil**

1 **onion**, chopped

2 **garlic cloves**, crushed

400 g (13 oz) **can chopped tomatoes**

150 ml (¼ pint) **white wine**

1 **red chilli**, deseeded and diced

375 g (12 oz) **tagliatelle**

400 g (13 oz) **mussels**, debearded and cleaned

250 g (8 oz) **crab meat (white and dark)**

4 tablespoons **lemon juice**

small handful of **parsley**, chopped

salt and **pepper**

Heat the oil in a frying pan over a medium heat, add the onion and garlic and cook for 3–4 minutes. Add the chopped tomatoes, white wine and chilli, season with salt and pepper and simmer for 8–9 minutes.

Cook the tagliatelle in a large pan of boiling water for 9–12 minutes, or according to packet instructions, until al dente.

Meanwhile, add the mussels to the tomato sauce, cover and cook for 4 minutes, until all the shells are open (discard any mussels that do not open).

Drain the tagliatelle and stir into the tomato sauce with the crab meat, lemon juice and parsley. Mix well and serve immediately.

For crab & mussel penne bake, cook 300 g (10 oz) penne in boiling water for 9–12 minutes, or according to packet instructions, until al dente. Meanwhile, heat 1 tablespoon olive oil in a pan over a medium heat, add 1 thinly sliced leek, 1 peeled and finely diced carrot, 1 diced celery stick and 2 crushed garlic cloves and cook for 4–5 minutes, until softened. Stir in 2 x 400 g (13 oz) cans of chopped tomatoes and 2 tablespoons shredded basil leaves and cook for 8–10 minutes. Stir in the cooked and drained pasta, 200 g (7 oz) dark and white crab meat and 100 g (3½ oz) shelled mussels. Pour into an ovenproof dish and sprinkle with 100 g (3½ oz) grated Emmental cheese. Cook under a preheated grill for 8–10 minutes, until golden and bubbling. Serve immediately. **Total cooking time 30 minutes.**

spicy tuna, tomato & olive pasta

Serves **4**
Total cooking time **20 minutes**

350 g (11½ oz) **penne**
2 x 400 g (13 oz) **cans tuna in spring water**, drained
2 **red chillies**, finely chopped
1 teaspoon **dried red chilli flakes**
200 g (7 oz) **pitted black olives**
240 g (8 oz) **sun-blush tomatoes in oil**
salt and **pepper**
chopped **flat leaf parsley**, to garnish

Cook the pasta in a large saucepan of lightly salted boiling water according to packet instructions until al dente.

Meanwhile, put the tuna in a large bowl and roughly flake with a fork, then add the red chillies, chilli flakes, olives and tomatoes with their oil.

Drain the pasta, add to the tuna mixture and toss to mix well, then season.

Spoon into warm bowls, scatter with chopped parsley and serve.

For spicy tuna, tomato & olive pasta salad, cook 200 g (10 oz) fresh penne in a large saucepan of lightly salted boiling water for 2–4 minutes, or according to the packet instructions, until al dente. Drain, then refresh under cold running water and drain again. Meanwhile, put 2 drained 400 g (12 oz) cans tuna in spring water in a salad bowl and roughly flake with a fork, then add 200 g (7 oz) pitted black olives, 2 roughly chopped plum tomatoes, 1 finely chopped red chilli and a small handful of chopped flat leaf parsley. Add the drained pasta, then drizzle over 1 tablespoon chilli oil and 2 tablespoons extra virgin olive oil and squeeze over the juice of 1 lemon. Season, toss to mix well and serve. **Total cooking time 10 minutes.**

midweek meals

prawn, tomato & feta rigatoni

Serves **4**
Total cooking time **20 minutes**

2 tablespoons **olive oil**
1 **onion**, finely chopped
2 **garlic cloves**, finely chopped
1 teaspoon **tomato purée**
juice of ½ **lemon**
1 teaspoon **sugar**
½ teaspoon **dried chilli flakes**
400 g (13 oz) **can chopped
    tomatoes**
200 g (7 oz) **frozen large raw
    peeled prawns**
400 g (13 oz) **rigatoni**
50 g (2 oz) **feta cheese**
salt and **pepper**
chopped **flat leaf parsley**, to
    garnish

Heat the oil in a saucepan, add the onion and garlic and cook for a couple of minutes until softened. Stir in the tomato purée, then add the lemon juice, sugar, chilli flakes and tomatoes. Bring to the boil, then reduce the heat and simmer for 10 minutes.

Remove the pan from the heat then, using a stick blender, whizz to a smooth purée. Return to the heat, add the prawns and cook for 3–5 minutes or until they have turned pink and are just cooked through and season well.

Meanwhile, cook the pasta in a large saucepan of salted boiling water according to packet instructions until al dente. Drain, reserving a little of the cooking water, and return to the pan. Stir through the prawn sauce, adding a little cooking water if needed. Spoon into serving bowls, then crumble over the feta and serve sprinkled with the parsley.

For prawn penne with no-cook tomato sauce & feta, cook 500 g (1 lb) fresh penne according to packet instructions until al dente. Add the prawns to the pan 5 minutes before the end of the cooking time and cook until they are pink and are cooked through. Meanwhile, mix 2 chopped and deseeded tomatoes, 1 tablespoon sweet chilli sauce and a handful of chopped basil leaves in a bowl. Drain the pasta and prawns and return to the pan. Drizzle with olive oil, mix in the tomato sauce and serve with 50 g (2 oz) crumbled feta cheese. **Total cooking time 10 minutes.**

bacon & tomato tortiglioni

Serves **4**
Total cooking time **20 minutes**

1 tablespoon **olive oil**
4 **streaky bacon rashers**
150 g (5 oz) **cherry tomatoes
on the vine**
325 g (11 oz) **tortiglioni**
50 g (2 oz) **rocket leaves**

**For the mascarpone
mayonnaise**
1 **egg yolk**
125 g (4 oz) **mascarpone
cheese**
50 ml (2 fl oz) **extra virgin
olive oil**
15 g (½ oz) **Parmesan
cheese**, grated
salt and **pepper**

Rub the oil on to a grill pan, add the bacon and cook under a preheated medium grill for 5–7 minutes until starting to crisp. Add the tomatoes. Shake the pan to coat in the oil, season and return to the grill. Cook for 5 minutes or until the bacon is cooked through and tomatoes are lightly charred. Meanwhile, cook the pasta in a saucepan of salted boiling water according to packet instructions until al dente.

Make the mascarpone mayonnaise. Place the egg yolk and mascarpone together in a food processor and whizz together. With the motor still running, add the oil through the funnel, one small drop at a time, until you get a smooth mayonnaise-like sauce. Stir in the Parmesan and season.

Drain the pasta, reserving a little cooking water, and return to the pan. Stir through a little of the mascarpone mixture, followed by the rocket. Add a little cooking water to loosen if needed. Spoon into bowls, dollop over the remaining mayonnaise and top with the bacon slices and tomato.

For quick tomato, Parma ham & rocket spaghettini, cook 325 g (11 oz) spaghettini in a large saucepan of salted boiling water according to packet instructions until al dente. Drain, then return to the pan. Stir through 3 tablespoons mascarpone cheese mixed with 15 g (½ oz) grated Parmesan cheese, 4 drained and chopped sun-dried tomatoes in oil and 4 slices of Parma ham, cut into strips. Serve sprinkled with plenty of chopped rocket leaves. **Total cooking time 10 minutes.**

spicy sardine linguine

Serves **4**

Total cooking time **20 minutes**

2 tablespoons **olive oil**

1 **red onion**, chopped

2 **garlic cloves**, crushed

400 g (13 oz) **can cherry tomatoes**

½ teaspoon **dried chilli flakes**

pinch of **sugar**

½ teaspoon finely grated **lemon** rind

350 g (11½ oz) **linguine**

2 x 120 g (3¾ oz) **cans sardines in oil**, drained

2 teaspoons **capers**, drained

salt and **pepper**

basil leaves, to garnish (optional)

Heat the olive oil in a large pan and cook the onion and garlic over a medium heat for 6–7 minutes, until softened. Add the tomatoes, chilli flakes, sugar, lemon rind and seasoning and bring to the boil. Cover and simmer for about 10 minutes, until thickened.

Meanwhile, cook the linguine in a large pan of boiling salted water for 11 minutes, or according to packet instructions, until al dente. Drain, reserving 2 tablespoons of the cooking water and return to the pan.

Stir the sardines and capers into the tomato sauce for the final 1–2 minutes. When hot, add to the drained pasta along with the reserved cooking water and toss gently. Serve heaped into bowls and garnished with extra black pepper, and with basil leaves, if liked.

For spicy tomato & sardine pasta bake, make the tomato sauce with sardines following the main recipe, but reducing the simmering time to 5 minutes so that the sauce is less thick. Meanwhile, cook 300 g (10 oz) penne in a large pan of boiling salted water until al dente. Stir into the sauce, tip into a large, ovenproof dish and top with 125 g (4 oz) halved mini mozzarella balls. Bake in a preheated oven, 200°C (400°F), Gas Mark 6, for 15–18 minutes, or until golden and bubbling. **Total cooking time 30 minutes.**

tortellini, pepper & rocket salad

Serves **4**
Total cooking time **10 minutes**

2 x 250 g (8 oz) **ready-made
  fresh spinach and ricotta
  tortellini**
400 g (13 oz) **roasted red
  and yellow peppers in oil
  (from a jar)**, drained
100 g (3½ oz) **rocket leaves**
1 **red onion**, thinly sliced
200 ml (7 fl oz) **fresh Italian-
  style salad dressing**
black pepper

Cook the tortellini according to packet instructions.

Meanwhile, chop the peppers and place in a bowl with the rocket leaves and onion. Add the cooked tortellini.

Pour over the salad dressing, toss to mix well and serve sprinkled with black pepper.

For red & yellow pepper tortellini, cut 1 red and 1 yellow pepper into large pieces, removing the seeds and membrane. Place skin side up under a hot grill until the skin blackens and blisters. Cool in a plastic bag, then peel away the skin. Roughly chop the white sections of 8 spring onions and place in a food processor with the peppers and 2 chopped garlic cloves and pulse until chopped. Cook 2 x 250 g (8 oz) ready-made fresh spinach and ricotta tortellini in a large saucepan of boiling water according to packet instructions. Drain and return to the pan. Toss the pepper mixture into the pasta, add 6 tablespoons olive oil and 40 g (1½ oz) grated Parmesan cheese. Season to taste. Garnish with extra spring onions and serve. **Total cooking time 30 minutes.**

chicken, chorizo & broccoli pasta

Serves **4**

Total cooking time **20 minutes**

250 g (8 oz) **rigatoni**

125 g (4 oz) **broccoli florets**

2 tablespoons **olive oil**

2 **skinless chicken breast fillets**, sliced

175 g (6 oz) **chorizo**, thickly sliced

200 ml (7 fl oz) **crème fraîche**

4 teaspoons chopped **parsley**

salt and **pepper**

freshly grated **Parmesan cheese**, to serve

Cook the rigatoni in lightly salted boiling water for 10 minutes, or according to packet instructions, until al dente, adding the broccoli for the final 5 minutes of the cooking time.

Meanwhile, heat the oil in a frying pan, add the chicken and chorizo and fry for 5–8 minutes or until the chicken is cooked through. Stir in the crème fraîche and heat through, then add the parsley. Add a little water if the sauce becomes too thick.

Add the pasta and broccoli and stir well to mix. Season with salt and pepper and serve with plenty of freshly grated Parmesan cheese.

For chicken, chorizo & leek lasagne, fry 2 chopped skinless chicken breast fillets, 175 g (6 oz) chopped chorizo and 1 sliced leek in 2 tablespoons olive oil over a high heat for 5 minutes. Stir in 350 g (11½ oz) ready-made tomato pasta sauce and heat through. Layer sheets of fresh lasagne and the tomato mixture in an ovenproof dish. Pour 350 g (11½ oz) ready-made fresh cheese sauce over the top and bake in a preheated oven, 200°C (400°F), Gas Mark 6, for 20 minutes until golden and bubbling. Serve with broccoli. **Total cooking time 30 minutes.**

spinach & blue cheese salad

Serves **4**

Total cooking time **10 minutes**

400 g (13 oz) cooked and
  cooled **macaroni**
50 g (2 oz) **baby spinach**
400 g (13 oz) halved **cherry
  tomatoes**
4 sliced **spring onions**
200 ml (7 fl oz) **ready-made
  blue cheese dressing**
salt and **pepper**

Place the cooked and cooled macaroni in a salad bowl
with the spinach, cherry tomatoes and spring onions.

Drizzle over the blue cheese dressing.

Season to taste, toss to mix well and serve immediately.

For macaroni cheese with spinach & tomatoes,
cook 275 g (9 oz) macaroni in a large saucepan of
boiling salted water for 8–10 minutes, or according to
packet instructions, drain well and set aside. Meanwhile,
melt 40 g (1½ oz) butter over a medium heat in a
heavy-based saucepan. Add 40 g (1½ oz) plain flour
and stir to form a roux, cooking for a few minutes. Warm
600 ml (1 pint) milk separately. Whisk in the warmed
milk, a little at a time. Cook for 10–15 minutes until the
sauce is thick and smooth. Stir in 100 g (3½ oz) finely
chopped baby spinach leaves and 100 g (3½ oz) cherry
tomatoes and season well. Remove from the heat, add
200 g (7 oz) grated Cheddar cheese and stir until the
cheese is well combined and melted. Add the macaroni
and mix well. Transfer to a deep ovenproof dish.
Sprinkle over a further 50 g (2 oz) Cheddar cheese and
place under a preheated hot grill. Cook until the cheese
is browned and bubbling. Serve immediately. **Total
cooking time 30 minutes.**

linguine with seafood

Serves **2**

Total cooking time **20 minutes**

3 tablespoons **olive oil**

2 **garlic cloves**, sliced

1 **red chilli**, deseeded if liked, and finely chopped

75 ml (3 fl oz) **dry white wine**

250 g (8 oz) **tomatoes**, deseeded and chopped

500 g (1 lb) **mussels**, debearded and cleaned

200 g (7 oz) **linguine**

handful of **flat leaf parsley**, chopped

salt and **pepper**

Heat the oil in a large saucepan, add the garlic and chilli and cook for a few seconds until beginning to colour. Pour in the wine and cook for a couple of minutes until the mixture is reduced by half. Stir in the tomatoes and cook for a further 5 minutes, adding a little water if needed.

Add the mussels to the pan, cover with a lid and cook for 5 minutes, shaking occasionally, until the mussels open. Discard any that remain closed.

Meanwhile, cook the pasta in a large saucepan of salted boiling water according to packet instructions until al dente. Drain, toss through the mussel sauce and season. Scatter over the parsley and serve immediately.

For Cajun-style seafood linguine, heat a little olive oil in a frying pan, add 150 g (5 oz) sliced smoked sausage and fry until golden. Add 1 chopped onion and cook until softened. Stir in 2 crushed garlic cloves and 1 teaspoon Cajun seasoning. Pour over a 400 g (13 oz) can chopped tomatoes and simmer for 20 minutes. Add the mussels, prepared as above, and continue as above. **Total cooking time 30 minutes.**

chicken & bacon pasta bake

Serves **4**

Total cooking time **20 minutes**

2 teaspoons **olive oil**

2 **boneless, skinless chicken breasts**

4 **back bacon rashers**

325 g (11 oz) **penne**

150 g (5 oz) **asparagus spears**, trimmed and thickly sliced

150 g (5 oz) **crème fraîche**

100 ml (3½ fl oz) **milk**

25 g (1 oz) **Parmesan cheese**, grated

salt and **pepper**

Rub the oil over the chicken breasts and season well, then cook under a preheated hot grill for 7 minutes on each side or until golden and cooked through. Add the bacon to the grill pan when you turn over the chicken and cook until just crisp. Cool slightly, then chop into bite-sized pieces.

Meanwhile, cook the pasta in a large saucepan of salted boiling water according to packet instructions until al dente. Add the asparagus 3 minutes before the end of the cooking time and cook until just tender. Drain well and return to the pan.

Mix together the crème fraîche and milk in a bowl, then stir into the pasta. Add the chicken and bacon and season well.

Spoon into a large heatproof dish and scatter the Parmesan on top. Cook under the hot grill for 5 minutes or until golden and heated through.

For asparagus & chicken penne with Parma ham, cook the penne as above. Meanwhile, drizzle a little olive oil and balsamic vinegar over 150 g (5 oz) trimmed asparagus spears. Season, then cook on a hot griddle for 5 minutes, turning frequently, until soft. Chop into pieces. Drain the pasta, reserving a little of the cooking water, and return to the pan. Toss through the asparagus, 1 ready-cooked roasted chicken breast, skin discarded and torn into strips, and 3 tablespoons crème fraîche. Serve topped with a slice of Parma ham. **Total cooking time 10 minutes.**

136

lemon & tuna conchiglie

Serves **4**
Total cooking time **20 minutes**

400 g (13 oz) **conchiglie**
1 **small garlic clove**, crushed
juice and grated rind of ½
    lemon
5 tablespoons **extra virgin**
    olive oil
225 g (7½ oz) **can tuna in oil**,
    drained
2 tablespoons **capers**, drained
large handful of **flat leaf**
    parsley, chopped
salt and **pepper**

Cook the pasta in a large saucepan of salted boiling water according to packet instructions until al dente.

Meanwhile, mix together the garlic, lemon juice and rind and olive oil in a bowl. Using a fork, break the tuna into large chunks and carefully stir into the dressing with the capers.

Drain the pasta, reserving a little of the cooking water, and return to the pan. Stir through the tuna and dressing, adding a little cooking water to loosen if needed. Season well, then stir in the parsley and serve immediately.

For fresh tuna, caper & lemon conchiglie, season 2 thick tuna steaks, rub all over with olive oil and place in an ovenproof dish. Place in a preheated oven, 110°C (225°F), Gas Mark ¼, for 20–25 minutes, depending how rare you like it. Meanwhile, cook and drain the conchiglie as above. Cut the fish into large chunks and toss through the pasta with a little chopped red onion, 2 tablespoons rinsed and drained capers, a squeeze of lemon juice and a handful of chopped flat leaf parsley. Serve immediately. **Total cooking time 30 minutes.**

bacon carbonara

Serves **4**
Total cooking time **20 minutes**

400 g (13 oz) **spaghetti**
25 g (1 oz) **butter**
3 **garlic cloves**, finely diced
2 **shallots**, finely diced
8 **streaky bacon rashers**,
  chopped
4 **eggs**
200 ml (7 fl oz) **single cream**
40 g (1½ oz) **Parmesan
  cheese**, grated

Cook the spaghetti in a saucepan of boiling water according to packet instructions, until al dente.

Meanwhile, heat the butter in a frying pan and fry the garlic, shallots and bacon for 5–7 minutes, until golden.

Beat together the eggs, cream and half the Parmesan.

Using tongs, transfer the cooked spaghetti to the frying pan – don't worry if some of the cooking liquid comes with it.

Pour in the egg mixture and toss the spaghetti until well coated, adding more cooking liquid if necessary. Serve sprinkled with the remaining Parmesan.

For bacon & pine nut pasta with poached eggs, bring a large saucepan of water to a gentle simmer and stir with a large spoon to create a swirl. Carefully break 2 eggs into the water and cook for 3 minutes. Remove with a slotted spoon and repeat with another 2 eggs. Keep them warm. Cook 400 g (13 oz) tagliatelle in a saucepan of boiling water according to packet instructions, until al dente. Meanwhile, heat 1 tablespoon olive oil in a frying pan and fry 175 g (6 oz) bacon rashers, cut into strips, for 2 minutes. Add 200 g (7 oz) frozen peas, 2 tablespoons vegetable stock, 4 tablespoons crème fraîche and 4 sliced spring onions. Stir well and bring to a gentle simmer. Continue to cook for 3–4 minutes. Drain the pasta, transfer to the frying pan and gently toss in the creamy bacon sauce. Divide the pasta between 4 shallow bowls and top each one with a poached egg. Serve sprinkled with 2 tablespoons grated Parmesan and pepper. **Total cooking time 30 minutes.**

delicatessen pasta salad

Serves **4**

Total cooking time **10 minutes**

2 x 250 g (8 oz) **packs ready-
made fresh spinach and
ricotta tortellini**

1 x 275 g (9 oz) **jar mixed
sliced roasted peppers in
olive oil**

1 x 275 g (9 oz) **jar
mushrooms in olive oil,**
drained

200 g (7 oz) **sun-blush
tomatoes**, drained

25 g (1 oz) **basil leaves**

50 g (2 oz) **rocket leaves**

black pepper

Bring a large pan of lightly salted water to the boil. Add
the tortellini and cook according to packet instructions.
Drain well and tip into a large bowl.

Add the jar of mixed peppers, including the oil, along
with the drained mushrooms and sun-blush tomatoes.

Add the basil leaves and rocket. Season with black
pepper, stir gently to combine and serve warm.

For Italian-style pasta broth, bring 1 litre (1¾ pint)
vegetable stock to the boil in a large saucepan and add
1 diced carrot, 1 diced onion and 1 diced celery stalk.
Bring back to the boil and cook for 10 minutes. Add
2 x 300 g (10 oz) packs of fresh spinach and ricotta
tortellini and cook for 3–4 minutes. Remove from the
heat and stir in 25 g (1 oz) each of chopped basil and
chopped rocket leaves and serve ladled into warmed
bowls. **Total cooking time 20 minutes.**

chicken pesto pasta

Serves **4**

Total cooking time **20 minutes**

375 g (12 oz) **penne**

large handful of **basil leaves**

25 g (1 oz) **toasted pine nuts**,
plus extra to serve

25 g (1 oz) freshly grated
Parmesan cheese, plus
extra to serve

1 **garlic clove**, peeled

3 tablespoons **olive oil**

175 g (6 oz) **ready-cooked
chicken**

handful of chopped **black
olives**

salt and **pepper**

Cook the penne in lightly salted boiling water for
10 minutes, or according to packet instructions, until
just al dente.

Meanwhile, make the pesto. Put the basil, pine nuts,
Parmesan, garlic and olive oil in a small food processor
or blender and process until almost smooth.

Drain the cooked penne and return to the pan. Add the
pesto, chicken and olives. Season with salt and pepper
and gently heat through. Serve sprinkled with extra pine
nuts and Parmesan.

For chicken pasta salad with pesto dressing, cook
250 g (8 oz) quick-cook pasta bows in lightly salted
boiling water for 5 minutes or until just tender. Drain,
rinse under running cold water and drain again. Mix
with 1 tablespoon ready-made pesto, 1 tablespoon
olive oil and 1 teaspoon balsamic vinegar. Add 200 g
(7 oz) ready-cooked chopped chicken, 8 halved cherry
tomatoes, 50 g (2 oz) baby spinach leaves and a
handful of toasted pine nuts. Lightly mix together and
serve. **Total cooking time 10 minutes.**

bucatini with sardines & fennel

Serves **4**

Total cooking time **20 minutes**

pinch of **saffron threads**

5 tablespoons **boiling water**

3 tablespoons **olive oil**

1 **garlic clove**, finely chopped

50 g (2 oz) **fresh white breadcrumbs**

400 g (13 oz) **bucatini pasta**

1 **onion**, chopped

1 **fennel bulb**, chopped

1 teaspoon **fennel seeds**

2 **anchovy fillets in oil**, drained

2 tablespoons **raisins**

4 **sardines**, boned and filleted

2 tablespoons **toasted pine nuts**

handful of **dill**, chopped

salt and **pepper**

Place the saffron in a small bowl and pour over the measurement water. Leave to stand for 5 minutes. Meanwhile, heat 1 tablespoon of the oil in a small frying pan, add the garlic and breadcrumbs and cook for a couple of minutes until golden. Set aside.

Cook the pasta in a large saucepan of salted boiling water according to packet instructions until al dente. Meanwhile, heat another tablespoon of the oil in a large frying pan, add the onion and both kinds of fennel and cook for 5 minutes to soften. Mash in the anchovies, then add the saffron with its soaking water. Add the raisins and let it bubble for 2 minutes.

Rub the remaining tablespoon of oil over the sardine fillets and season well. Cook on a preheated hot griddle pan or under a hot grill for 3 minutes on each side or until cooked through. Drain the pasta, reserving a little of the cooking water, and return to the pan. Toss through the sauce, adding a little cooking water to loosen if needed. Season well. Spoon on to serving plates, top with the sardine fillets. Serve scattered with the pine nuts, breadcrumbs and dill.

For quick sardine spaghettini, cook 400 g (13 oz) spaghettini according to packet instructions until al dente. Meanwhile, place a 120 g (4 oz) can sardines in tomato sauce and 1 chopped tomato in a small saucepan and heat through. Stir in 1 tablespoon rinsed and drained capers. Drain the pasta, reserving some cooking water, and return to the pan. Stir through the sauce, adding a little cooking water to loosen, and serve immediately. **Total cooking time 10 minutes.**

spanish seafood pasta

Serves **4**
Total cooking time **20 minutes**

2 tablespoons **olive oil**
1 **onion**, finely chopped
1 **garlic clove**, crushed
1 teaspoon **tomato purée**
1 teaspoon **paprika**
125 ml (4 fl oz) **dry white wine**
400 g (13 oz) **can chopped tomatoes**
1 litre (1¾ pints) hot **chicken stock**
300 g (10 oz) **angel hair pasta**
200 g (7 oz) **mussels**, debearded and cleaned
125 g (4 oz) **large cooked unpeeled prawns**
75 g (3 oz) **prepared squid rings**, cleaned

Heat the oil in a large saucepan, add the onion and garlic and cook over a medium heat for 5 minutes or until softened. Stir in the tomato purée and paprika, then pour over the wine and bubble for 1–2 minutes until reduced a little. Pour in the tomatoes and stock and bring to the boil.

Break the pasta into small lengths about 2.5 cm (1 inch) long. Reduce the heat so the mixture is simmering and stir the pasta into the pan. Cover with a lid and cook for 7 minutes, stirring occasionally to stop the pasta from sticking.

Add the mussels, cover and cook for 3 minutes until the mussels begin to open. Add the prawns and squid rings and cook for a further 2 minutes or until the seafood is cooked through and all the mussels have opened. Discard any mussels that remain closed.

Bring the pan to the table and serve.

For Spanish seafood pasta with chicken, rub a little olive oil over 2 boneless chicken breasts and place in a roasting tin. Cook in a preheated oven, 200°C (400°F), Gas Mark 6, for 20 minutes or until cooked through. Meanwhile, make the recipe as above. Cut the chicken into slices, discarding the skin, and add to the pan with the squid for the last 2 minutes of cooking. **Total cooking time 30 minutes.**

salmon & leek cannelloni

Serves **4**

Total cooking time **30 minutes**

500 ml (17 fl oz) hot
  vegetable or **fish stock**
3 **leeks**, thinly sliced
2 **salmon fillets**, about 150 g
  (5 oz) each, cut into chunks
200 g (7 oz) **crème fraîche**
8 **fresh lasagne sheets**
50 g (2 oz) **dried
  breadcrumbs**
salt and **pepper**

Pour half the hot stock over the leeks in a saucepan and boil for 5 minutes until soft. Pour the remaining stock over the salmon in a separate saucepan and simmer for 5 minutes until the fish flakes easily. Drain both, reserving the stock. Mix the stock with the crème fraîche. Flake the fish, discarding the skin and any bones.

Stir together the leeks and salmon with 6 tablespoons of the crème fraîche mixture to loosen, then season. Place some of the mixture along one long side of a lasagne sheet. Roll up and place, seam-side down, in a baking dish. Repeat with the remaining lasagne sheets. Pour over the remaining crème fraîche mixture and sprinkle with the breadcrumbs.

Place in a preheated oven, 200°C (400°F), Gas Mark 6, for 15–20 minutes until golden and cooked through.

For leek and salmon linguine, cook 400 g (13 oz) linguine according to packet instructions, adding 3 thinly sliced leeks for the last 5 minutes of cooking. Drain and then stir through 100 g (3½ oz) chopped smoked salmon and 5 tablespoons crème fraîche. **Total cooking time 10 minutes.**

linguine with spicy lamb sauce

Serves **4**

Total cooking time **20 minutes**

2 tablespoons **olive oil**
4 **lamb chops**, boned
400 g (13 oz) **linguine**
2 **garlic cloves**, sliced
1 **red chilli**, deseeded if liked,
   and sliced
50 ml (2 fl oz) **dry white wine**
salt and **pepper**
chopped **mint leaves**, to
   garnish

Brush a little of the oil over the lamb chops, season well and cook under a preheated hot grill for 5–7 minutes on each side or until golden and just cooked through. Trim away the fat and cut into thin slices.

Meanwhile, cook the pasta in a large saucepan of salted boiling water according to packet instructions until al dente.

Heat a saucepan and add the remaining oil. Add the garlic and chilli and gently fry for 1 minute until the garlic is golden, then pour over the wine and cook until reduced by half. Season well.

Drain the pasta and return to the pan, then toss through the sauce and lamb slices and season. Spoon into serving bowls and serve sprinkled with the mint.

For linguine with stir-fried lamb, cook the linguine as above. Meanwhile, cut 2 lamb chops into thin strips. Heat 2 tablespoons olive oil in a wok or large frying pan, add the lamb strips and 2 sliced garlic cloves and stir-fry for 5 minutes or until just cooked through. Add 75 g (3 oz) pitted black olives 1 minute before the end of the cooking time. Squeeze over the juice of 1 lemon and stir in a handful of chopped mint leaves. Drain the pasta and return to the pan. Toss through the lamb and olives and serve immediately. **Total cooking time 10 minutes.**

penne arrabbiata

Serves **4**

Total cooking time **20 minutes**

4 tablespoons **olive oil**

2 **red chillies**, finely sliced

2 **garlic cloves**, chopped

600 g (1¼ lb) **canned chopped tomatoes**

6–8 **basil leaves**, shredded

400 g (13 oz) **penne**

salt and **pepper**

25 g (1 oz) **Parmesan cheese**, grated, to serve

Heat the olive oil in a large frying pan, add the red chillies and garlic and cook for 2–3 minutes.

Add the chopped tomatoes and basil and simmer for 12 minutes. Season to taste.

Meanwhile, cook the penne in a saucepan of boiling water according to packet instructions, until al dente. Drain the pasta and add it to the tomato sauce. Stir until combined.

Serve sprinkled with grated Parmesan.

For quick spicy tomato pasta, heat 2 tablespoons olive oil in a large frying pan and sauté 1 diced shallot and 1 finely diced red chilli, until softened, then add 3–4 chopped plum tomatoes and 1 tablespoon chopped basil leaves. Meanwhile, cook 300 g (10 oz) fresh conchiglie in a saucepan of boiling water according to the packet instructions, until al dente, then drain. Remove the tomato mixture from the heat and stir in the pasta and 1 tablespoon balsamic vinegar. Place 60 g (2¼ oz) watercress on a serving platter and spoon over the tomato pasta. Serve sprinkled with 2 tablespoons grated mozzarella cheese and 2 tablespoons toasted pine nuts. **Total cooking time 10 minutes.**

pork & mushroom pasta

Serves **4**

Total cooking time **30 minutes**

2 tablespoons **olive oil**
1 **onion**, finely chopped
1 **garlic clove**, finely chopped
450 g (14½ oz) **pork mince**
1 tablespoon **tomato purée**
250 ml (8 fl oz) **dry white wine**
150 ml (¼ pint) hot **chicken stock**
150 g (5 oz) **mushrooms**, trimmed and chopped
75 ml (3 fl oz) **double cream**
400 g (13 oz) **lumaconi pasta**
25 g (1 oz) **Parmesan cheese**, grated, plus extra to serve
salt and **pepper**
chopped **flat leaf parsley**, to garnish

Heat 1 tablespoon of the oil in a large frying pan, add the onion and cook for a couple of minutes until beginning to soften. Add the garlic and pork and cook, breaking up the meat with the back of a spoon, for 5–10 minutes or until the meat is golden.

Stir in the tomato purée and cook for a further 1 minute. Pour over the wine and cook until reduced by half, then add the chicken stock and simmer for 10 minutes.

Heat the remaining oil in a separate frying pan. Add the mushrooms and cook for 3 minutes or until golden and soft. Add to the pork, then stir in the cream.

Meanwhile, cook the pasta in a large saucepan of salted boiling water according to packet instructions until al dente. Drain, reserving a little of the cooking water, and return to the pan. Stir through the sauce and Parmesan, adding a little cooking water to loosen if needed. Season well.

Spoon into serving bowls and serve sprinkled with the parsley and extra Parmesan.

For mushroom & Parma ham pasta, cook and drain 400 g (13 oz) penne. Meanwhile, fry the mushrooms as above, adding 1 chopped garlic clove. When golden, stir through the pasta with the grated rind and juice of 1 lemon and 6 slices of Parma ham, torn into strips. Toss through a handful of rocket leaves, if liked. Serve immediately. **Total cooking time 10 minutes.**

penne with walnut sauce

Serves **4**

Total cooking time **20 minutes**

2 tablespoons **olive oil**
3 **shallots**, diced
150 g (5 oz) **walnut pieces**
350 g (11½ oz) **penne**
2 tablespoons **mascarpone cheese**
3 tablespoons **natural yogurt**
2 tablespoons chopped **parsley**
pepper
30 g (1¼ oz) **Parmesan cheese**, grated, to serve

Heat the olive oil in a frying pan and sauté the shallots for 2–3 minutes.

Place half the walnuts in a food processor or blender and process until fine.

Add the remaining walnuts to the frying pan and cook for 5–6 minutes.

Meanwhile, cook the penne in a saucepan of boiling water according to packet instructions, until al dente.

Stir the ground walnuts, mascarpone and yogurt into the frying pan and stir until smooth. Stir in the chopped parsley and simmer gently for a few minutes.

Drain the pasta, reserving 2 tablespoons of the cooking liquid. Add the pasta and liquid to the walnut sauce and toss together gently. Add pepper to taste.

Serve sprinkled with grated Parmesan.

For walnut penne pesto, cook 400 g (13 oz) penne according to packet instructions, until al dente. Meanwhile, put 175 g (6 oz) walnut pieces and 1 crushed garlic clove in a food processor or blender and process until finely chopped. Add a handful of basil leaves, 100 g (3½ oz) grated Parmesan, 2 teaspoons lemon juice and 4 tablespoons olive oil and process again until nearly smooth. Add a little more olive oil if needed to loosen the mixture. Drain the pasta and serve with the pesto. **Total cooking time 10 minutes.**

kale & pecorino pesto linguini

Serves **4**

Total cooking time **20 minutes**

375 g (12 oz) **linguini**

300 g (10 oz) **kale**

2 tablespoons **olive oil**

3 **garlic cloves**, crushed

100 g (3½ oz) **toasted pine nuts**

100 g (3½ oz) **mascarpone cheese**

100 g (3½ oz) **pecorino cheese**, grated, plus extra shavings to garnish

½ teaspoon grated **nutmeg**

salt and **pepper**

Cook the pasta according to packet instructions until al dente.

Meanwhile, wash the kale well, remove any tough stems and chop roughly.

Heat the oil in a pan and sauté the garlic for 2–3 minutes. Add the kale to the pan. Cover and cook for 2–3 minutes, or until the kale starts to wilt.

Place the pine nuts into a food processor or blender and whizz until smooth. Tip in the mascarpone, pecorino and nutmeg. Whizz again.

Add the kale and garlic mixture and whizz until smooth. Season to taste.

Drain the pasta and return it to the pan. Add the pesto and toss to mix well. Serve the pasta garnished with shavings of pecorino.

For kale & pecorino pasta frittata, mix together 400 g (13 oz) cooked linguini with 4 beaten eggs and 10 tablespoons kale and pecorino pesto (from the recipe above). Season well. Preheat the grill to medium-high. Heat 2 tablespoons olive oil in a large frying pan and add the pasta mixture. Flatten the mixture with a spoon and cook over a medium heat for 8–10 minutes then place under the preheated grill for 4–5 minutes or until golden. Serve immediately with a crisp green salad. **Total cooking time 30 minutes.**

tuna & bean pasta salad

Serves **2**
Total cooking time **20 minutes**

150 g (5 oz) **penne**
75 g (3 oz) **green beans**,
 trimmed and halved
200 g (7 oz) **can tuna in
 sunflower oil**, drained and
 broken into chunks
200 g (7 oz) **canned kidney
 beans**, rinsed and drained
50 g (2 oz) **antipasti roasted
 peppers from a jar**, drained
 and chopped
2 **spring onions**, chopped
1 tablespoon balsamic vinegar
½ teaspoon **Dijon mustard**
3 tablespoons **olive oil**
salt and **pepper**

Cook the penne in a saucepan of lightly salted boiling water for 10 minutes, or according to packet instructions, until al dente, adding the green beans for the final 5 minutes. Drain and rinse under cold running water, then drain again.

Place the pasta and green beans in a bowl with the tuna, kidney beans, peppers and spring onions.

Whisk together the vinegar, mustard and oil in a small bowl. Season, then pour the dressing over the salad and toss lightly to mix.

For Niçoise pasta salad with egg, cook 150 g (5 oz) penne in a saucepan of lightly salted boiling water for 10 minutes, or until just tender, adding 75 g (3 oz) trimmed green beans for the final 5 minutes. Drain and rinse under cold running water, then drain again. In a separate small saucepan, boil 2 eggs for 8 minutes, then drain and leave to cool in cold water. Arrange the pasta and beans on a serving plate. Add a 200 g (7 oz) can tuna, drained and broken into chunks, 2 tomatoes, cut into wedges, and 8 black olives. Shell the eggs, cut in half and place on the salad. Mix together 1 tablespoon balsamic vinegar, ½ teaspoon Dijon mustard and 3 tablespoons olive oil in a bowl. Season and drizzle over the salad. **Total cooking time 30 minutes.**

spaghetti puttanesca

Serves **4**

Total cooking time **20 minutes**

1 tablespoon **olive oil**

4 **garlic cloves**, thinly sliced

2 x 400 g (13 oz) **cans
chopped tomatoes**

2 tablespoons **capers**, drained

4 **anchovy fillets**, chopped

a handful of **green olives**,
pitted and sliced

1 teaspoon **dried chilli flakes**

a small handful of **parsley**,
roughly chopped

400 g (13 oz) **spaghetti**

Heat the olive oil in a saucepan and cook the garlic for
1 minute, then add the tomatoes, capers, anchovies,
olives and chilli flakes. Simmer for 10 minutes, until the
sauce starts to thicken. Stir in the chopped parsley.

Meanwhile, cook the spaghetti in a saucepan of boiling
water according to packet instructions, until al dente.
Drain the pasta, toss in the sauce and serve.

For Sicilian anchovy spaghetti, halve 6 plum tomatoes,
put in a roasting tin and roast for 15 minutes in a
preheated oven, 200°C (400°F), Gas Mark 6. Cook
350 g (11½ oz) spaghetti in a saucepan of boiling
water according to packet instructions, until al dente.
Meanwhile, heat 1 tablespoon olive oil in a frying
pan and fry 3 eggs until the white is set but the yolk
is still runny. Chop the tomatoes roughly and stir in
4 chopped anchovy fillets, 1 chopped garlic clove,
1 tablespoon chopped gherkins and 50 g (2 oz)
breadcrumbs. Chop the eggs and add to the mixture.
Drain the pasta and stir into the sauce with 1 tablespoon
olive oil and 1 tablespoon chopped parsley. Serve
immediately sprinkled with 2 tablespoons grated
Parmesan cheese. **Total cooking time 30 minutes.**

mexican chicken tagliatelle

Serves **4**
Total cooking time **30 minutes**

3 tablespoons **olive oil**
1 **onion**, finely chopped
2 **garlic cloves**, finely chopped
1 tablespoon **tomato purée**
400 g (13 oz) **can chopped tomatoes**
1 teaspoon **chipotle paste** or **chipotle sauce**
2 **boneless, skinless chicken breasts**
400 g (13 oz) **tagliatelle**
salt and **pepper**

To serve
chopped **fresh coriander leaves**, to garnish
50 ml (2 fl oz) **soured cream**

Heat 2 tablespoons of the oil in a saucepan, add the onion and cook for 3 minutes, stirring often. Then add the garlic and cook for 2–3 minutes or until softened. Stir in the tomato purée, tomatoes and chipotle paste or sauce. Simmer for 20 minutes, adding a little water if needed, then season.

Meanwhile, rub the remaining oil over the chicken breasts and season well. Heat a griddle pan until smoking, add the chicken and cook for 7 minutes on each side or until lightly charred and cooked through. Alternatively, cook under a preheated hot grill.

Cook the pasta in a large saucepan of salted boiling water according to packet instructions until al dente. Drain, reserving a little cooking water. Stir through the tomato sauce, adding a little cooking water to loosen if needed.

Cut the chicken into bite-sized pieces and stir through the pasta. Spoon into serving bowls, sprinkle with the fresh coriander and serve with dollops of soured cream.

For fiery chicken pasta salad, cook 500 g (1 lb) fresh penne according to packet instructions until al dente. Drain, then cool under cold running water and drain again. Meanwhile, chop 5 deseeded tomatoes, 2 spring onions, ½ red chilli, deseeded if liked, and mix in a bowl with a squeeze of lime juice and a drizzle of extra virgin olive oil. Tip the pasta in a serving dish and mix well with the tomato mixture and 1 ready-cooked roasted chicken breast, skin discarded and flesh shredded. **Total cooking time 10 minutes.**

mussel & courgette rigatoni

Serves **4**

Total cooking time **20 minutes**

1.5 kg (3 lb) **mussels**,
  debearded and cleaned
200 ml (7 fl oz) **white wine**
400 g (13 oz) **rigatoni**
2 tablespoons **olive oil**
1 **onion**, diced
2 **garlic cloves**, crushed
2 **courgettes**, sliced

To serve

3 tablespoons grated
  Parmesan cheese
2 tablespoons **chopped
  chives**

Place the mussels and wine in a large saucepan and cook over a high heat for 5–6 minutes, until the mussels open. Drain, reserving the cooking liquid, and remove the mussels from their shells. Discard any mussels that have not opened.

Cook the rigatoni in a saucepan of boiling water according to packet instructions, until al dente.

Meanwhile, heat the olive oil in a saucepan and sauté the onion and garlic for 2–3 minutes, then add the courgettes and cook for a further 4–5 minutes.

Drain the pasta and stir into the courgettes with the mussels and strained mussel cooking liquid.

Serve immediately sprinkled with grated Parmesan and chopped chives.

For rigatoni, mussel & feta salad, cook 350 g (11½ oz) rigatoni in a saucepan according to packet instructions, until al dente, adding 150 g (5 oz) frozen peas 1 minute before the end of cooking. Meanwhile, mix 200 g (7 oz) crumbled feta with 50 g (2 oz) rocket, the grated rind of 1 lemon, 1 grated courgette, 2 tablespoons chopped mint and 20 smoked mussels. Drain the pasta and peas and refresh under cold water. Toss with the other ingredients and add 2 tablespoons extra virgin olive oil and the juice of ½ lemon. Season and serve. **Total cooking time 10 minutes.**

anchovy & rocket spaghetti

Serves **4**

Total cooking time **20 minutes**

75 g (3 oz) **ciabatta bread**
1 tablespoon **olive oil**
1 **garlic clove**, crushed
400 g (13 oz) **spaghetti**
50 g (2 oz) **rocket leaves**
salt and **pepper**

For the anchovy sauce
8 **anchovy fillets in oil**,
   drained
3 tablespoons **mascarpone
   cheese**
juice of ½ **lemon**
1 **egg**, lightly beaten
25 g (1 oz) **Parmesan
   cheese**, grated

Place the ciabatta in a food processor or blender and whizz to form chunky breadcrumbs. Heat the oil in a small frying pan, add the garlic and stir around the pan, then add the breadcrumbs. Cook for 5–7 minutes until golden and crisp all over, then remove from the pan and set aside.

Make the anchovy sauce. Mash the anchovies on a board, using the back of a large knife, to form a paste. Place in a bowl and mix in the mascarpone, then stir in the lemon juice, egg and Parmesan.

Cook the pasta in a large saucepan of salted boiling water according to packet instructions until al dente. Drain, reserving a little of the cooking water, and return to the pan. Stir in the anchovy sauce and mix together well, adding a little cooking water to loosen if needed. Season, then toss through the rocket leaves.

Spoon into serving bowls and serve scattered with the breadcrumbs.

For spaghetti with buttery anchovy, lemon & rocket sauce, cook and drain the spaghetti as above. Meanwhile, place 8 drained anchovy fillets in oil, 50 g (2 oz) softened butter, the grated rind of 1 lemon and 75 g (3 oz) rocket leaves in a food processor or blender and whizz together. Stir the butter through the drained pasta and serve immediately. **Total cooking time 10 minutes.**

chorizo & red pepper pasta

Serves **2**
Total cooking time **10 minutes**

200 g (7 oz) **rocchetti pasta**
1 tablespoon **olive oil**, plus
    extra to serve
75 g (3 oz) **chorizo**, thinly
    sliced
1 **red pepper**, cored,
    deseeded and cut into
    chunks
1 **garlic clove**, crushed
1 tablespoon **tomato purée**
75 ml (3 fl oz) **dry white wine**
teaspoon **sugar**
salt and **pepper**
chopped **flat leaf parsley**, to
    garnish

Cook the pasta in a large saucepan of salted boiling water according to packet instructions until al dente.

Meanwhile, heat the oil in a large frying pan, add the chorizo slices and cook, for a couple of seconds until crisp. Remove with a slotted spoon and set aside.

Add the red pepper to the pan and cook for a couple of minutes until browned. Stir in the garlic and tomato purée and cook for a further 30 seconds. Pour over the wine, add the sugar and stir well. Bring to the boil, then cook for 5 minutes until reduced slightly and season.

Drain the pasta and return to the pan. Toss with a little olive oil, then stir through the chorizo and sauce. Spoon into serving bowls and serve sprinkled with the parsley.

For pasta with rich red pepper sauce, place the red pepper chunks and 3 halved tomatoes in a roasting tin and drizzle with a little olive oil and a splash of white wine. Place in a preheated oven, 190°C (375°F), Gas Mark 5, for 20–25 minutes. Meanwhile, cook and drain the fiorelli as above. Sprinkle the pepper and tomatoes with 1 teaspoon smoked paprika, then toss through the drained pasta. Serve with dollops of soured cream. **Total cooking time 30 minutes.**

tomato & sweet potato ravioli

Serves **4**

Total cooking time **20 minutes**

50 g (2 oz) **butter**

375 g (12 oz) peeled **sweet potato**, cut into 1 cm (½ in) cubes

2 **garlic cloves**, chopped

small handful of **sage leaves**, chopped

grated zest of ½ **lemon**, plus a squeeze of juice

200 g (7 oz) **cherry tomatoes**, halved

2 x 250 g (8 oz) **packs ready-made fresh cheese-filled ravioli**

salt and **pepper**

To serve

100 g (3½ oz) **soft goats' cheese**, crumbled

large handful **rocket leaves**

Melt half the butter in a large frying pan, add the chopped sweet potato, season well, then fry over a medium heat for about 5–6 minutes until golden brown all over.

Add the garlic, sage and lemon zest and fry together for 1 minute. Add the remaining butter, the cherry tomatoes and the lemon juice and gently fry over a low heat for 1 minute until melted.

Meanwhile, cook the ravioli according to packet instructions. Drain, then drizzle with a little olive oil and add the cooked pasta to the pan with the sweet potato and cherry tomatoes. Carefully stir to coat with the sauce.

Spoon into serving bowls and scatter with the goats' cheese, rocket leaves and black pepper before serving.

For rocket, tomato & ravioli pasta salad, cook 2 x 250 g (8 oz) packs ready-made fresh cheese-filled ravioli according to packet instructions, drain under cold water and then place in a wide salad bowl with a large handful of rocket, 100 g (3½ oz) crumbled goats' cheese and 200 g (7 oz) halved cherry tomatoes. Whisk together 6 tablespoons olive oil with 1 crushed garlic clove and the juice of 1 lemon. Season, pour over the salad and toss to mix well before serving. **Total cooking time 10 minutes.**

pepper & spinach gratin

Serves **4**
Total cooking time **20 minutes**

350 g (11½ oz) **pappardelle**
1 **red pepper**, cored,
    deseeded and cut into
    chunks
1 **yellow pepper**, cored,
    deseeded and cut into
    chunks
2 tablespoons **olive oil**
100 g (3½ oz) **black olives**,
    pitted and roughly chopped
4 tablespoons **capers**, drained
250 g (8 oz) **baby spinach
    leaves**
300 g (10 oz) **mozzarella
    cheese**, cubed
4 tablespoons grated
    Parmesan cheese

Cook the pappardelle in a large saucepan of lightly
salted boiling water for 8–10 minutes, or according to
packet instructions, until al dente.

Meanwhile, place the peppers in a roasting tin and
toss with the oil. Cook under a preheated hot grill for
5 minutes, turning until lightly charred and soft.

Drain the pasta and return to the pan with the olives,
capers, spinach and mozzarella and toss over a low
heat for 1 minute until the spinach wilts and the
mozzarella starts to melt. Add the grilled peppers with
the oil and toss.

Pile into 4 flameproof serving bowls and sprinkle
each with Parmesan, then place under the hot grill for
1 minute until the tops are golden. Serve hot.

For antipasti pepper, caper & spinach pasta, cook
600 g (1¼ lb) fresh pappardelle in a large saucepan of
lightly salted boiling water for 3 minutes, or according
to packet instructions. Drain well, then add 2 x 280 g
(9 oz) jars antipasti peppers, drained, 75 g (3 oz) pitted
and chopped black olives and 4 tablespoons drained
capers. Toss well and heat for 2 minutes until piping hot.
Season well and serve with 2 handfuls of baby spinach
leaves stirred through. **Total cooking time 10 minutes.**

food for
friends

fiery black spaghetti with squid

Serves **4**

Total cooking time **10 minutes**

400 g (13 oz) **black squid ink
    spaghetti**
4 tablespoons **olive oil**, plus
    extra to serve
400 g (13 oz) **prepared squid**,
    cleaned and sliced into rings
4 **garlic cloves**, sliced
1 **red chilli**, deseeded, if liked,
    and sliced
juice and rind of 1 **lemon**
handful of **basil leaves**,
    chopped
handful of **baby plum
    tomatoes**, halved
salt and **pepper**

Cook the pasta in a large saucepan of salted boiling
water according to packet instructions until al dente.

Meanwhile, heat the oil in a large frying pan. Pat the
squid rings dry with kitchen paper, then add to the pan
and cook over a high heat for about 30 seconds until
starting to brown. Add the garlic and chilli and cook for
a couple of seconds, taking care not to let the garlic
burn. The squid should be white and just cooked through.
Squeeze over the lemon juice and season to taste.

Drain the pasta and return to the pan. Toss through
the squid and add olive oil to taste. Serve immediately,
sprinkled with the baby plum tomatoes, basil and
lemon rind.

For lemony black spaghetti with seared squid,
heat a little butter in a saucepan, add 1 finely chopped
shallot and 3 sliced garlic cloves and cook gently until
soft. Squeeze over the juice of 1 lemon, then, over a low
heat, whisk in 50 g (2 oz) cold butter, cubed. Sprinkle
with a handful of torn basil leaves and set aside. Cook
the squid ink spaghetti as above. Cut 8 prepared and
cleaned small squid in half. Lightly score each half to
make a criss-cross pattern. Toss in a little olive oil and
salt. Cook on a preheated hot griddle pan for 2 minutes,
turning until charring and curling up. Drain the pasta,
toss through the lemon sauce. Serve with the squid and
sprinkle with dried chilli flakes and extra chopped basil.
Total cooking time 20 minutes.

creamy seafood lasagne

Serves **4**

Total cooking time **30 minutes**

325 g (11 oz) **shop-bought fresh tomato pasta sauce**

pinch of **chilli flakes**

200 g (7 oz) **skinless cod fillet**, cut into bite-sized pieces

200 g (7 oz) **cooked peeled small prawns**

100 g (3½ oz) **ready-cooked shelled mussels**

olive oil, for oiling

300 g (10 oz) **fresh lasagne sheets**

200 ml (7 fl oz) **crème fraîche**

5 tablespoons **milk**

25 g (1 oz) **Parmesan cheese**, grated

Heat the tomato sauce in a small saucepan together with the chilli flakes and cod until warmed through. Add the prawns and mussels.

Spoon a little of the seafood mixture over the bottom of a lightly oiled baking dish. Cover with a layer of lasagne sheets. Spoon over half the remaining seafood mixture. Mix together the crème fraîche and milk to make a smooth sauce, then drizzle one-quarter over the ingredients in the baking dish. Cover with another layer of pasta. Repeat until you have 3 layers of pasta, then pour over the remaining crème fraîche sauce and scatter with the Parmesan.

Place in a preheated oven, 200°C (400°F), Gas Mark 6, for 15–20 minutes until golden and cooked through.

For creamy prawn and tomato linguine, cook 500 g (1 lb) fresh linguine according to packet instructions with 200 g (7 oz) raw peeled large prawns – the prawns will need about 3 minutes to cook through. Drain and stir through 100 g (3½ oz) halved cherry tomatoes, 4 tablespoons mascarpone cheese and a handful of chopped basil, then serve. **Total cooking time 10 minutes.**

salsa verde chicken spaghetti

Serves **4**

Total cooking time **20 minutes**

1 tablespoon **olive oil**
2 **boneless, skinless chicken breasts**
400 g (13 oz) **spaghetti**
salt and **pepper**

For the salsa verde
large handful of **flat leaf parsley**
small handful of **basil leaves**
1 **garlic clove**, crushed
5 tablespoons **extra virgin olive oil**
grated rind of 1 **lemon**, plus a squeeze of lemon juice
1–2 tablespoons **capers**, drained

Rub the oil over the chicken breasts and season well. Cook under a preheated hot grill for 7 minutes on each side or until golden and cooked through.

Meanwhile, cook the pasta in a large saucepan of salted boiling water according to packet instructions until al dente.

To make the salsa verde, place the herbs, garlic, oil, lemon rind and juice in a small food processor or blender. Pulse for a couple of seconds, then add the capers and pulse a few more times to form a thick paste.

Drain the pasta, reserving a little of the cooking water, and return to the pan. Stir through the salsa verde, adding a little cooking water to loosen if needed, and season.

Cut the chicken into thick slices. Spoon the pasta on to serving plates and serve topped with the sliced chicken.

For simple chicken & salsa verde pasta salad, cook 500 g (1 lb) fresh penne according to packet instructions until al dente. Meanwhile, make the salsa verde as above. Drain the pasta, then cool under cold running water and drain again. Tip into a serving dish and stir through the salsa verde. Add 2 ready-cooked roasted chicken breasts, skin discarded and flesh torn into shreds, and 3 drained and chopped sun-dried tomatoes in oil. **Total cooking time 10 minutes.**

linguine with chicory & pancetta

Serves **2**

Total cooking time **20 minutes**

1 tablespoon **olive oil**

50 g (2 oz) cubed **pancetta**

1 **small onion**, sliced

1 **garlic clove**, sliced

2 **red chicory**, trimmed and
   sliced

50 ml (2 fl oz) **dry white wine**

50 ml (2 fl oz) hot **chicken
   stock**

200 g (7 oz) **linguine**

25 g (1 oz) **mascarpone
   cheese**

15 g (½ oz) **Parmesan
   cheese**, grated, plus extra
   to serve

salt and **pepper**

Heat the oil in a frying pan, add the pancetta and cook until it begins to colour. Add the onion and cook for 5 minutes or until it begins to soften and turn golden.

Add the garlic and cook for 30 seconds, then stir in the chicory. Cook for a few minutes until it wilts, then pour over the wine. Cook until reduced by half, then pour over the stock and simmer for 7 minutes.

Meanwhile, cook the pasta in a large saucepan of salted boiling water according to packet instructions until al dente. Drain, reserving a little of the cooking water and return to the pan.

Stir the mascarpone and Parmesan into the sauce, season well and toss through the pasta, adding a little cooking water to loosen if needed. Spoon on to serving plates and serve scattered with extra Parmesan.

For roasted chicory, pancetta & mascarpone linguine, halve 4 heads of chicory and place in a roasting tin. Dab with a little butter and then pour over 100 ml (3½ fl oz) chicken stock. Place in a preheated oven, 180°C (350°F), Gas Mark 4, for 20–25 minutes or until golden and soft. Meanwhile, cook and drain the linguine and fry the pancetta, onion and garlic as above. Cut the roasted chicory into thin wedges and stir through the pasta with the pancetta mixture, mascarpone and Parmesan as above. **Total cooking time 30 minutes.**

asparagus & herb pappardelle

Serves **4**

Total cooking time **30 minutes**

450 g (14½ oz) **asparagus**,
   trimmed and cut into 2.5 cm
   (1 inch) lengths
400 g (13 oz) **pappardelle**
1 tablespoon **olive oil**
1 **onion**, diced
2 **garlic cloves**, crushed
300 ml (½ pint) **single cream**
¼ teaspoon grated **nutmeg**
2 tablespoons each of
   chopped **basil, parsley** and
   chives
2 tablespoons grated
   Parmesan cheese, to serve

Blanch the asparagus in a saucepan of boiling water for 3–4 minutes. Drain and keep warm.

Cook the pappardelle in a saucepan of boiling water according to packet instructions, until al dente.

Meanwhile, heat the olive oil in a frying pan and sauté the onion and garlic for 4–5 minutes.

Stir in the cream and simmer for 6–8 minutes, until the cream has reduced and thickened a little. Stir in the grated nutmeg.

Drain the pasta and add to the cream sauce with the asparagus and herbs. Toss together gently.

Serve sprinkled with grated Parmesan.

For asparagus pesto pasta, cook 400 g (13 oz) tagliatelle in a saucepan of boiling water according to packet instructions, until al dente. Meanwhile, cook 500 g (1 lb) trimmed asparagus in a saucepan of boiling water for 2–3 minutes, then drain. Place the asparagus, 125 g (4 oz) spinach leaves, 30 g (1¼ oz) grated Parmesan cheese, 2 crushed garlic cloves and 2 tablespoons toasted pine nuts in a food processor and blitz for 30 seconds, then pour in 3–4 tablespoons extra virgin olive oil with the motor still running until a thick paste forms. Add the juice of ½ lemon and a little water to loosen and season to taste. Drain the pasta, return to the pan and add the asparagus pesto. Toss together. Serve sprinkled with extra toasted pine nuts. **Total cooking time 20 minutes.**

clam crème fraîche linguine

Serves **4**

Total cooking time **10 minutes**

2 tablespoons **olive oil**

3 **garlic cloves**, sliced

½ **red chilli**, finely chopped

100 ml (3½ fl oz) **dry white wine**

1 kg (2 lb) cleaned **live clams**

500 g (1 lb) **fresh linguine**

100 g (3½ oz) **crème fraîche**

salt and **pepper**

handful of **flat leaf parsley**, chopped, to garnish

Heat the oil in a large saucepan. Add the garlic and chilli and cook for a few seconds. Pour in the wine and bring to the boil. Add the clams, then reduce the heat, cover the pan and cook for 5 minutes until they have opened. Discard any that remain closed.

Meanwhile, cook the pasta according to packet instructions. Drain, reserving some of the cooking water, and return to the pan.

Stir the pasta into the clams with the crème fraîche, adding a little of the reserved cooking water to loosen the mixture if necessary. Season, then scatter over the parsley to serve.

For clam linguine pasta parcels, cook 400 g (13 oz) dried linguine for 3 minutes less than instructed on the pack. Drain. Cook 3 crushed garlic cloves and ½ finely chopped red chilli briefly in 2 tablespoons olive oil. Add 50 ml (2 fl oz) dry white wine and 100 g (3½ oz) crème fraîche, then toss with the pasta. Divide between 4 pieces of lightly oiled foil. Top with 500 g (1 lb) cleaned live clams. Seal tightly, leaving a little air around the clams. Place on a baking sheet in a preheated oven, 200°C (400°F), Gas Mark 6, for 5–8 minutes until the clams have opened, discarding any that remain closed. **Total cooking time 20 minutes.**

creamy courgette orzo pasta

Serves **4**

Total cooking time **30 minutes**

375 g (12 oz) **orzo** (rice-shaped pasta)

1 tablespoon **butter**

1 tablespoon **olive oil**

1 **red chilli**, deseeded and finely chopped

2 **garlic cloves**, finely chopped

4 **spring onions**, very finely chopped

3 **courgettes**, coarsely grated

finely grated zest of 1 small **unwaxed lemon**

150 g (5 oz) **soft cheese with garlic and herbs**

4 tablespoons finely chopped **flat leaf parsley**

salt and **pepper**

Bring a large pan of lightly salted water to the boil, then cook the pasta according to packet instructions.

Meanwhile, heat the butter and olive oil in a large frying pan, then add the chilli, garlic, spring onions and courgettes. Cook over a medium-low heat for 10–15 minutes, or until softened, stirring often.

Reduce the heat and add the lemon zest. Cook gently for 3–4 minutes, add the soft cheese and mix thoroughly. Season to taste.

Drain the pasta and add to the courgette mixture. Stir in the parsley, mix well and serve immediately.

For minted courgette, cherry tomato & orzo pasta salad, cook 375 g (12 oz) orzo according to packet instructions. Meanwhile, place 2 coarsely grated courgettes, 4 sliced spring onions, 4 tablespoons finely chopped mint leaves and 200 g (7 oz) halved cherry tomatoes in a wide salad bowl. Make a dressing by whisking together 1 finely chopped red chilli, 2 crushed garlic cloves, 6 tablespoons olive oil, the juice of 1 lemon and 1 teaspoon honey. Season well. Drain the pasta and rinse under cold running water until cool. Drain again and add to the salad bowl. Pour over the dressing and toss to mix well before serving. Total cooking time 20 minutes.

tagliatelle with pumpkin & sage

Serves **4**

Total cooking time **30 minutes**

875 g (1¾ lb) **pumpkin,
butternut** or **winter squash,**
peeled, deseeded and cut
into 1.5 cm (¾ in) cubes
4 tablespoons **olive oil**
500 g (1 lb) **tagliatelle**
50 g (2 oz) **rocket leaves**
8 **sage leaves**, chopped
grated **Parmesan cheese**, to
serve (optional)
salt and **pepper**

Place the pumpkin into a small roasting tin, add 2
tablespoons of the olive oil, season and toss to mix well.
Roast in a preheated oven, 220°C (425°F), Gas Mark 7,
for 15–20 minutes or until just tender.

Meanwhile, bring a large pan of salted water to the
boil. Cook the pasta according to packet instructions.
Drain, return to the pan, then add the rocket, sage
and pumpkin. Mix together over a gentle heat with the
remaining olive oil until the rocket has wilted, then serve
with a good grating of fresh Parmesan cheese, if liked.

For cheat's pumpkin & sage ravioli, cook 2 x 250 g
(8 oz) packs ready-made fresh pumpkin-filled ravioli
according to packet instructions. Meanwhile, heat
4 tablespoons butter and 4 tablespoons olive oil in
a large frying pan with 2 chopped garlic cloves and
6 sage leaves over a medium low heat. Drain the ravioli
and add to the pan. Season and toss gently to mix
well and serve, sprinkled with 100 g (3½ oz) grated
Parmesan cheese. **Total cooking time 10 minutes.**

light clam & tomato broth

Serves **4**
Total cooking time **20 minutes**

150 g (5 oz) **tomatoes**
2 tablespoons **olive oil**
2 **garlic cloves**, finely chopped
150 ml (¼ pint) **dry white
wine**
2 litres (3½ pints) hot **chicken
or fish stock**
5 **sun-dried tomatoes in oil**,
drained and finely chopped
200 g (7 oz) **anellini pasta**
1 kg (2 lb) **clams**, cleaned
salt and **pepper**
chopped **flat leaf parsley**, to
garnish

To serve
lemon wedges
crusty bread

Cut a cross at the stem end of each tomato, place in
a heatproof bowl and pour over boiling water to cover.
Leave for 1–2 minutes, then drain and peel off the skins.
Halve the tomatoes, remove the seeds and roughly chop.

Heat the oil in a large saucepan, add the garlic and
cook for 30 seconds until beginning to turn golden.
Pour over the wine and cook for 5 minutes until slightly
reduced. Pour over the stock and bring to the boil. Add
the fresh and sun-dried tomatoes, season and simmer
for 5 minutes.

Add the pasta and clams, cover with a lid and cook for
5 minutes until the pasta has cooked through and the
clams have opened. Discard any that remain closed.
Season to taste.

Ladle into serving bowls, sprinkle with the parsley and
serve with lemon wedges and crusty bread.

For simple spaghetti with clams, heat a little olive oil
in a large saucepan, add 1 finely chopped garlic clove
and 1 chopped red chilli and cook for 1 minute until
softened. Pour over 75 ml (3 fl oz) dry white wine and
add the cleaned clams as above. Cover and cook for
5 minutes until the clams have opened. Discard any that
stay closed. Meanwhile, cook 400 g (13 oz) quick-cook
spaghetti according to packet instructions until al dente.
Drain and return to the pan. Toss through the clams and
their cooking liquid, 3 tablespoons crème fraîche and
a handful of chopped flat leaf parsley. **Total cooking
time 10 minutes.**

tuna sashimi & rocket linguine

Serves **2**
Total cooking time **30 minutes**

150 g (5 oz) **very fresh tuna steak**
200 g (7 oz) **linguine**
3 tablespoons **extra virgin olive oil**, plus extra to serve
juice of ½ **lemon**
50 g (2 oz) **rocket leaves**
salt and **pepper**
Parmesan cheese shavings, to serve

Wrap the tuna tightly in clingfilm and place in the freezer for 20 minutes and then, using a sharp knife, slice into very thin strips.

Meanwhile, cook the pasta in a large saucepan of salted boiling water according to packet instructions until al dente. Drain the pasta and return to the pan, then toss through the tuna with 1 tablespoon each of olive oil and lemon juice.

Toss together the rocket and remaining lemon juice and 1 tablespoon oil in a bowl and season.

Spoon the pasta into serving bowls, arrange the rocket salad on top and grind over plenty of black pepper. Serve scattered with the Parmesan shavings and drizzled with the remaining olive oil.

For wintery tuna & rocket linguine, cook the linguine as above. Meanwhile, mix together 1 egg yolk, the juice and grated rind of 1 lemon and 1 crushed garlic clove in a bowl. Drain the pasta and return to the pan. Stir through the egg mixture, 160 g (5½ oz) canned tuna, drained and flaked, a handful of rinsed and drained capers and 50 g (2 oz) rocket leaves. Serve immediately. **Total cooking time 10 minutes.**

duck & pancetta mafaldine

Serves **4**

Total cooking time **30 minutes**

3 tablespoons **olive oil**
1 **onion**, finely chopped
1 **carrot**, peeled and finely
  chopped
1 **celery stick**, finely chopped
1 **garlic clove**, crushed
1 tablespoon **tomato paste**
75 ml (3 fl oz) **dry white wine**
400 g (13 oz) **can chopped
  tomatoes**
2 strips of **orange** peel
200 ml (7 fl oz) **water**
1 **bay leaf**
1 **thyme sprig**
100 g (3½ oz) **pancetta
  cubes**
4 **confit duck legs**
400 g (13 oz) **mafaldine**
salt and **pepper**

Heat 2 tablespoons of the oil in a large saucepan, add the onion, carrot and celery and cook gently for 5 minutes until softened. Stir in the garlic and tomato paste and cook for a further 1 minute.

Pour over the wine, increase the heat and bubble vigorously for a couple of minutes until reduced, then stir in the tomatoes, orange peel and measurement water. Add the herbs, bring to the boil and cook for 15 minutes.

Remove the pan from the heat. Remove the orange peel and herbs then, using a stick blender, whizz to form a smooth sauce. Return to the heat.

Meanwhile, heat the remaining oil in a frying pan, add the pancetta and cook until golden. Using a fork, tear the duck into shreds, then add to the sauce with the pancetta and simmer for 5 minutes.

Cook the pasta in a large saucepan of salted boiling water while the sauce is cooking, according to packet instructions, until al dente. Drain, reserving a little of the cooking water, and return to the pan. Stir through the sauce, adding a little cooking water to loosen if needed. Season to taste and serve immediately.

For quick confit duck & red pepper mafaldine,

cook and drain the mafaldine as above. Meanwhile, cut 4 confit duck legs and 2 drained roasted red peppers from a jar into bite-sized pieces. Toss the duck and peppers through the drained pasta with 5 tablespoons crème fraîche and 125 g (4 oz) watercress. Serve immediately. **Total cooking time 10 minutes.**

chicken & dolcelatte pasta bake

Serves **2**

Total cooking time **30 minutes**

2 tablespoons **olive oil**

1 **small onion**, chopped

175 g (6 oz) **skinless chicken breast fillets**, chopped

150 ml (¼ pint) **double cream**

75 ml (3 fl oz) **dry white wine**

1 teaspoon **wholegrain mustard**

175 g (6 oz) **penne**

125 g (4 oz) **broccoli florets**

75 g (3 oz) **dolcelatte cheese**, chopped

25 g (1 oz) **fresh breadcrumbs**

salt and **pepper**

green salad, to serve

Heat 1 tablespoon of the oil in a frying pan, add the onion and cook for 2 minutes, then add the chicken and cook for a further 5 minutes until cooked through. Stir in the cream, wine and mustard and simmer for 5 minutes.

Meanwhile, cook the pasta in a saucepan of lightly salted boiling water for 10 minutes, or until just tender, adding the broccoli for the final 5 minutes. Drain, add to the sauce and stir well to coat. Add the cheese, stir well and season.

Tip the mixture into an ovenproof dish, sprinkle over the breadcrumbs and drizzle over the remaining oil. Bake in a preheated oven, 200°C (400°F), Gas Mark 6, for 15 minutes until golden and bubbling. Serve with a green salad.

For chicken & dolcelatte tagliatelle, heat

1 tablespoon olive oil in a frying pan, add 175 g (6 oz) chicken mini-fillets and fry for 2 minutes until golden. Add 150 ml (¼ pint) double cream, 75 ml (3 fl oz) dry white wine and 1 teaspoon wholegrain mustard and simmer for 5 minutes until the chicken is cooked through. Meanwhile, cook 250 g (8 oz) fresh egg tagliatelle and 75 g (3 oz) frozen peas in a saucepan of lightly salted boiling water for 3 minutes, or until just tender. Add 75 g (3 oz) chopped dolcelatte cheese to the sauce and stir until melted, then season. Drain the tagliatelle, add to the sauce and lightly stir to coat.
Total cooking time 10 minutes.

zingy crab vermicelli

Serves **4**
Total cooking time **10 minutes**

400 g (13 oz) **vermicelli**
250 g (8 oz) **fresh white crabmeat**
6 tablespoons **crème fraîche**
juice and grated rind of
   ½ **lemon**
1 **red chilli**, deseeded and
   finely chopped
handful of **flat leaf parsley**,
   chopped
salt and **pepper**

Cook the pasta in a large saucepan of salted boiling water according to packet instructions until al dente. Drain, reserving a little of the cooking water, and return to the pan.

Stir through the remaining ingredients, adding a little cooking water to loosen if needed, and season well. Serve immediately.

For crab & proscuitto vermicelli, heat a little olive oil in a frying pan, add 1 finely chopped shallot and cook over a low heat until softened. Add 1 sliced garlic clove and cook for a further 1 minute, then add 150 g (5 oz) diced proscuitto and cook over a medium heat for a couple of minutes until golden. Pour over 100 ml (3½ fl oz) dry white wine and cook until reduced. Stir through the crème fraîche and crabmeat as above and heat through. Meanwhile, cook and drain the vermicelli as above, then stir through the sauce. Serve immediately. **Total cooking time 20 minutes.**

vodka & tomato tacconelli

Serves **4**
Total cooking time **20 minutes**

15 g (½ oz) **butter**
8 **pancetta slices**
1 **rosemary sprig**
75 ml (3 fl oz) **vodka**
350 ml (12 fl oz) **shop-bought tomato pasta sauce**
400 g (13 oz) **tacconelli pasta**
150 ml (¼ pint) **double cream**
salt and **pepper**
grated **Parmesan cheese**, to serve

Heat the butter in a saucepan, add the pancetta and cook for about 3 minutes until golden and crispy. Remove from the pan and keep warm. Stir in the rosemary, then remove from the heat and pour over the vodka. Return to a high heat and cook until the vodka has reduced down to 1 tablespoon. Pour over the tomato pasta sauce, reduce the heat and simmer for 10 minutes.

Meanwhile, cook the pasta in a large saucepan of salted boiling water according to packet instructions until al dente.

Remove the rosemary from the sauce, then stir in the cream. Drain the pasta, reserving some of the cooking water, and return to the pan. Stir through the sauce, adding a little of the cooking water to loosen if needed, and season.

Spoon into serving bowls, top with the pancetta slices and serve scattered with the Parmesan.

For quick vodka & tomato penne, cook 500 g (1 lb) fresh penne as above. Meanwhile, heat a little olive oil in a frying pan, add 3 tablespoons tomato purée and cook for 30 seconds. Add 100 g (3½ oz) halved baby plum tomatoes and 2 tablespoons vodka and cook for a couple of minutes until the tomatoes have softened, then stir in 150 ml (¼ pint) cream. Drain the pasta and return to the pan. Toss through the sauce and serve immediately. **Total cooking time 10 minutes.**

salmon & courgette pasta

Serves **4**
Total cooking time **20 minutes**

150 ml (¼ pint) **dry white wine**
150 g (5 oz) **crème fraîche**
a squeeze of **lemon juice**
handful of **dill**, chopped
12 **lasagne sheets**
2 **courgettes**
4 **hot-smoked salmon fillets**
3 **spring onions**, sliced
salt and **pepper**

Bring the wine to the boil in a small saucepan and boil for 5 minutes until syrupy and reduced by half. Add the crème fraîche, a squeeze of lemon juice and most of the dill. Season, then stir until mixed through.

Meanwhile, cook the lasagne sheets in a large saucepan of salted boiling water for 3–5 minutes or until soft, then drain well. Shave the courgettes into long thin strips using a vegetable peeler.

Cut each lasagne sheet into large irregular shapes and place in a bowl. Break the salmon into large chunks.

Arrange the salmon and pasta on serving plates with the courgette ribbons. Drizzle over the sauce and serve sprinkled with the spring onions and the remaining dill.

For courgette & salmon lasagne, prepare 12 fresh lasagne sheets, if necessary, according to packet instructions. Make the wine sauce as above, then grate 2 courgettes and stir into the sauce with the flaked salmon fillets. Layer up the sauce and lasagne sheets in an ovenproof dish, finishing with a layer of lasagne. Mix together 200 g (7 oz) crème fraîche and 100 g (3½ oz) ricotta cheese in a bowl and thin with milk to make a sauce. Pour over the lasagne, sprinkle with 25 g (1 oz) grated Parmesan, then place in a preheated oven, 200°C (400°F), Gas Mark 6, for about 15 minutes or until golden and bubbling. **Total cooking time 30 minutes.**

monkfish & fennel spaghetti

Serves **4**

Total cooking time **20 minutes**

3 tablespoons **boiling water**

½ teaspoon **saffron threads**

15 g (1½ oz) **butter**

1 **fennel bulb**, sliced

50 ml (2 fl oz) **dry white wine**

450 g (14½ oz) **mussels**,
debearded and cleaned

150 g (5 oz) **crème fraîche**

1 tablespoon **olive oil**

300 g (10 oz) **monkfish fillet**,
boned and cut into 1.5 cm
(¾ inch) thick slices

400 g (13 oz) **spaghetti**

salt and **pepper**

chopped **tarragon leaves**, to
garnish

Pour the measurement water over the saffron in a
heatproof bowl and leave to infuse.

Heat the butter in a large saucepan, add the fennel and
cook over a medium heat for 5 minutes until softened.
Pour over the wine and saffron with the soaking liquid
and add the mussels. Cover with a lid and cook for
5 minutes until the mussels have opened. Discard
any that remain closed. Stir through the crème fraîche
and season.

Meanwhile, heat the oil in a nonstick frying pan, add
the monkfish and cook over a high heat for 3 minutes
on each side or until just cooked through. Carefully stir
the monkfish into the mussel sauce.

Cook the pasta in a large saucepan of salted boiling
water, while the mussel sauce is cooking, according to
packet instructions until al dente. Drain, reserving a little
of the cooking water. Stir through the mussel sauce,
adding a little cooking water if needed, and season.

Spoon into serving bowls and serve sprinkled with
the tarragon.

For quick monkfish spaghetti, cook the monkfish,
prepared as above, under a preheated hot grill for
3–5 minutes on each side. Meanwhile, cook and drain
400 g (13 oz) quick-cook spaghetti as above. Stir
through the monkfish, 1 chopped tomato, ½ chopped
red chilli, deseeded if liked, a squeeze of lemon juice
and a handful of chopped flat leaf parsley. Serve
immediately. **Total cooking time 10 minutes.**

summery sausage pasta

Serves **4**

Total cooking time **30 minutes**

4 tablespoons **olive oil**
6 **large pork sausages**
2 **onions**, sliced
2 **red peppers**, cored,
  deseeded and sliced
2 **yellow peppers**, cored,
  deseeded and sliced
1 **garlic clove**, crushed
1 tablespoon **tomato purée**
2 teaspoons **sugar**
1 tablespoon **balsamic
  vinegar**
3 **large tomatoes**, chopped
2 tablespoons **water**
handful of **basil leaves**,
  chopped, plus extra to
  garnish
400 g (13 oz) **radiatore pasta**
salt and **pepper**

Grease a baking sheet with 1 tablespoon of the oil, add the sausages and place in a preheated oven, 200°C (400°F), Gas Mark 6, for 20–25 minutes, until brown and cooked through.

Meanwhile, heat the remaining oil in a saucepan, add the onions and cook for 5 minutes until softened. Add the peppers, garlic, tomato purée, sugar, vinegar, tomatoes and measurement water. Cover and cook for 15 minutes. Remove the lid and cook for a further 5 minutes until the peppers are really soft. Season well and stir through the basil.

Cook the pasta in a large saucepan of salted boiling water, while the sausages and peppers are cooking, according to packet instructions until al dente. Drain, reserving a little of the cooking water, and return to the pan.

Slice the sausages into bite-sized pieces. Stir through the pasta with the peppers, adding a little cooking water to loosen if needed. Season well. Spoon into serving bowls and serve sprinkled with extra chopped basil.

For winter sausage pasta, steam ½ head of thinly sliced cabbage over a saucepan of boiling water for 10 minutes until soft. Meanwhile, cook 400 g (13 oz) fusilli according to packet instructions until al dente. Drain the pasta and return to the pan. Stir through the cabbage, 3 smoked sausages (such as kielbasa), sliced, a knob of butter and 25 g (1 oz) grated Parmesan cheese. Serve immediately. **Total cooking time 10 minutes.**

sea bass with warm pasta salad

Serves **4**

Total cooking time **20 minutes**

2 tablespoons **olive oil**

4 **small sea bass fillets**,
  boned

300 g (10 oz) **fregola pasta**

squeeze of **lemon juice**

75 g (3 oz) **sun-blush
  tomatoes in oil**, drained and
  chopped

50 g (2 oz) **pitted black olives**

salt and **pepper**

For the basil oil

100 ml (3½ fl oz) **extra virgin
  olive oil**

large handful of **basil leaves**,
  roughly chopped

1 **garlic clove**

Make the basil oil. Place the extra virgin olive oil in a small saucepan, add the basil and garlic and cook over a low heat for 10 minutes. Leave to cool, then pass the flavoured oil through a sieve.

Heat the oil in a large nonstick frying pan, add the sea bass, skin side down, and cook over a high heat for 5–7 minutes until golden and crisp. Carefully turn over, season well and cook for a further 3–5 minutes or until the fish is opaque and cooked through. Slice each fillet in half.

Meanwhile, cook the pasta in a large saucepan of salted boiling water according to packet instructions until al dente. Drain well. Stir in 2 tablespoons of the basil oil, a good squeeze of lemon juice, the tomatoes and olives and season.

Arrange the fish alongside the pasta salad on serving plates and drizzle over the remaining basil oil.

For olive & pesto pasta with pan-fried sea bass,
cook the fregola pasta as above. Meanwhile, cut 4 boned sea bass fillets into thin strips and fry in a little olive oil in a frying pan for 3 minutes on each side or until just cooked through. Drain the pasta and return to the pan. Stir through 4 tablespoons shop-bought fresh green pesto and a handful of pitted black olives. Pile the pasta into serving bowls, arrange the fish strips on top and then scatter over 1 chopped tomato. Serve immediately. **Total cooking time 10 minutes.**

pasta, pine nut & butternut gratin

Serves **2**
Total cooking time **30 minutes**

250 g (8 oz) **butternut
squash**, peeled, deseeded
and sliced
1 tablespoon **olive oil**
2 **garlic cloves**, unpeeled
25 g (1 oz) **pine nuts**
250 g (8 oz) **pack ready-
made fresh four cheese
tortelloni**
150 ml (¼ pint) **double cream**
25 g (1 oz) grated **Parmesan
cheese**
4 tablespoons **fresh white
breadcrumbs**
4 **sage leaves**
salt and **pepper**
rocket and tomato salad, to
serve (optional)

Place the squash on a baking sheet, drizzle over the oil
and season. Roast in a preheated oven, 200°C (400°F),
Gas Mark 6, for 5 minutes. Add the garlic and pine
nuts, return to the oven and cook for a further 15–20
minutes until the squash is tender, the garlic is soft and
the pine nuts are toasted.

Cook the tortelloni in a saucepan of lightly salted
boiling water towards the end of the squash cooking
time, for 3–4 minutes, or according to packet
instructions, until al dente. Drain, tip into a flameproof
dish with the roasted squash and pine nuts and gently
toss together.

Squeeze the soft garlic from its skin, mix with the
cream and season. Spoon over the tortelloni and
squash and sprinkle with the Parmesan, breadcrumbs
and sage leaves. Place under a preheated medium grill
for 2–3 minutes until golden and bubbling. Serve with
a rocket and tomato salad, if liked.

For creamy pumpkin & pine nut stuffed pasta, cook
a 250 g (8 oz) pack ready-made fresh pumpkin and
pine nut pasta in a saucepan of lightly salted boiling
water for 3–4 minutes until tender. Meanwhile, in a
separate saucepan, heat 150 ml (¼ pint) double cream
and 1 crushed garlic clove. Season and stir in 50 g
(2 oz) baby spinach leaves. Drain the pasta and mix
with the sauce. Serve sprinkled with grated Parmesan
cheese. **Total cooking time 10 minutes.**

pepper & goats' cheese lasagne

Serves **4**

Total cooking time **30 minutes**

butter, for greasing

2 **ready-roasted red peppers**, chopped

handful of chopped **basil**

500 ml (17 fl oz) **ready-made tomato pasta sauce**

125 g (4 oz) **soft, rindless goats' cheese**

150 g (5 oz) **mascarpone cheese**

5 tablespoons **milk**

8 **fresh lasagne sheets**

75 g (3 oz) **ricotta cheese**

25 g (1 oz) **Parmesan cheese**, grated

salt and **pepper**

Lightly grease an ovenproof dish. Stir the red peppers and basil into the tomato sauce. In a separate bowl mix together the goats' cheese, mascarpone and milk and season to taste.

Pour one-quarter of the tomato sauce in the ovenproof dish, then top with one-third of the goats' cheese mixture. Arrange a layer of pasta sheets on top. Repeat the layers until you have 3 layers of pasta, then spread the remaining tomato sauce on top.

Spoon the ricotta over the sauce and scatter over the Parmesan. Place in a preheated oven, 200°C (400°F), Gas Mark 6, for 20–25 minutes until the pasta is tender.

For spaghetti with red peppers & goats' cheese,

cook 500 g (1 lb) quick-cook spaghetti in a large saucepan of lightly salted boiling water according to packet instructions. Meanwhile, mix 2 chopped ready-roasted red peppers with 125 g (4 oz) soft goats' cheese, 50 g (2 oz) mascarpone cheese and a good handful of chopped parsley. Drain the pasta, return to the pan and stir in the sauce. Season to taste and serve sprinkled with toasted flaked almonds and chopped basil. **Total cooking time 10 minutes.**

creamy chicken carbonara

Serves **4**

Total cooking time **10 minutes**

500 g (1 lb) **fresh linguine**

2 **ready-cooked chicken breasts**, torn into strips

1 **egg**, lightly beaten

4 tablespoons **crème fraîche**

finely grated rind of ½ **lemon**, plus 1 tablespoon juice

25 g (1 oz) **Parmesan cheese**, grated

salt and **pepper**

handful of chopped **chives**, to garnish

Cook the linguine in a large saucepan of lightly salted boiling water according to packet instructions. Drain, reserving a little of the cooking water, and return the pasta to the pan.

Add the chicken to the pan with the egg, crème fraîche, lemon rind and juice and half the Parmesan.

Season to taste and stir together, adding a little of the cooking water to loosen if necessary. Divide between bowls and sprinkle with the remaining Parmesan and the chives. Serve immediately.

For penne with creamy pan-fried chicken & lardons,

heat 1 tablespoon olive oil in a large, heavy-based saucepan. Add 50 g (2 oz) lardons and cook until golden. Remove from the pan and set aside. Add 4 chicken breast fillets to the pan and cook for 5 minutes on each side. Return the lardons to the pan along with 50 ml (2 fl oz) hot chicken stock and 50 ml (2 fl oz) double cream. Stir in 300 g (10 oz) fresh penne and simmer for 3 minutes until the pasta is al dente and the chicken is cooked through. Stir in 50 g (2 oz) frozen peas and 2 tablespoons lemon juice and heat through. Season to taste and serve sprinkled with chopped chives. **Total cooking time 20 minutes.**

macaroni prawn gratin

Serves **6**
Total cooking time **30 minutes**

3 **egg yolks**
juice of **1 lemon**
200 g (7 oz) **butter**, melted
100 ml (3½ fl oz) **double cream**
625 g (1¼ lb) **macaroni**
3 tablespoons **olive oil**
3 **leeks**, trimmed, cleaned and sliced
300 g (10 oz) **large cooked peeled prawns**
salt and **pepper**

Place the egg yolks in a heatproof bowl that will snugly fit over a saucepan of simmering water (make sure the bottom of the bowl doesn't touch the water). Add most of the lemon juice then, very slowly, start to pour in the butter, whisking continuously. As the butter thickens the sauce, you can add it a little quicker. When the sauce has thickened and is the consistency of mayonnaise, remove from the pan. Leave to cool, season well and add more lemon juice to taste. Whip the cream until soft peaks form, then carefully fold into the sauce.

Meanwhile, cook the pasta in a large saucepan of salted boiling water according to packet instructions until al dente.

Heat the oil in a saucepan, add the leeks with a splash of water and cook gently for about 7 minutes until beginning to soften. Add the prawns and cook for 2 minutes or until heated through.

Drain the pasta and return to the pan, then mix through the sauce, leeks and prawns and season. Spoon into individual gratin dishes and cook under a preheated hot grill for 3–5 minutes or until lightly browned all over.

For quick prawn & leek pasta, cook the leeks and prawns as above. Meanwhile, cook 625 g (1¼ lb) chifferi pasta according to packet instructions until al dente. Drain and return to the pan. Stir through the prawn mixture, 5 tablespoons crème fraîche and a good squeeze of lemon juice. Serve sprinkled with chopped basil. **Total cooking time 10 minutes.**

individual bacon pasta frittatas

Serves **4**

Total cooking time **30 minutes**

6 **streaky bacon rashers**

325 g (11 oz) **quick-cook spaghetti**

5 **eggs**, beaten

125 ml (4 fl oz) **single cream**

50 g (2 oz) **Gruyère cheese**, grated

handful of **flat leaf parsley**, chopped, to garnish

butter, for greasing

salt and **pepper**

Cook the bacon under a preheated medium grill for 7 minutes until cooked through. Cool, then cut into small pieces.

Meanwhile, cook the pasta in a large saucepan of salted boiling water according to packet instructions until al dente. Drain, then cool under cold running water and drain again. Cut into 2.5 cm (1 inch) lengths.

Mix together the eggs, cream and most of the cheese in a large bowl and season well. Stir in the cut pasta and bacon.

Grease a 12-hole muffin tin. Spoon a little of the mixture into each hole until nearly to the top. Sprinkle over the remaining cheese, then place in a preheated oven, 200°C (400°F), Gas Mark 6, for 15–20 minutes or until the mixture is just set. Serve sprinkled with parsley.

For caramelized onion & Parma ham spaghetti, heat a little olive oil in a frying pan, add 1 sliced onion and 1 sliced garlic clove and cook over a low heat for 15–20 minutes until soft and golden. Meanwhile, cook the spaghetti as above. Drain well and return to the pan. Stir 2 tablespoons crème fraîche and 4 slices of Parma ham, cut into small strips, into the onions, then toss through the pasta. Serve immediately. **Total cooking time 20 minutes.**

creamy lobster fettuccine

Serves **2**
Total cooking time **30 minutes**

25 g (1 oz) **butter**
2 **shallots**, finely chopped
1 teaspoon **tomato purée**
1 **large cooked lobster**
2 tablespoons **brandy**
150 ml (¼ pint) **Madeira**
75 ml (3 fl oz) **double cream**
1 **egg yolk**
pinch of **cayenne pepper**
200 g (7 oz) **fettuccine**
salt and **pepper**
chopped **tarragon leaves**, to
   garnish

Heat the butter in a large frying pan, add the shallots and cook over a low heat until softened. Stir in the tomato purée and cook for 1 minute. Meanwhile, remove the lobster meat from the shell and cut the tails in half. Add the lobster shell to the frying pan and cook for 5–10 minutes until browned.

Remove the pan from the heat and add the brandy. Return to the heat, pour over the Madeira and bubble for 5–10 minutes until reduced by half. Pass through a sieve, pressing down hard to extract the juices.

Return the sauce to the pan. Mix together the cream, egg yolk and cayenne pepper. Add a tablespoon of the sauce to the cream mixture to warm a little, then stir the cream into the pan. Heat through but do not let it boil, then add the lobster meat.

Meanwhile, cook the pasta in a large saucepan of salted boiling water according to packet instructions until al dente. Drain, reserving a little of the cooking water, and return to the pan. Toss the sauce through the pasta until coated all over, adding a little cooking water to loosen if needed, and season.

Spoon into serving bowls, top with the lobster tail and serve sprinkled with the tarragon.

For quick lobster fettuccine, cook the fettuccine as above. Drain, reserving a little of the cooking water, and return to the pan. Stir through 200 g (7 oz) potted lobster, 1 egg yolk and a handful of chopped tarragon leaves and serve immediately. **Total cooking time 10 minutes.**

pasta cakes with salmon & eggs

Serves **4**

Total cooking time **20 minutes**

300 g (10 oz) **angel hair pasta**

6 tablespoons **olive oil**

4 **eggs**

3 tablespoons **mascarpone cheese**

handful of grated **Parmesan cheese**

4 slices **smoked salmon**, cut into thin strips

salt and **pepper**

thinly sliced **chives**, to garnish

Cook the pasta in a large saucepan of salted boiling water according to packet instructions. Drain, then cool under cold running water and drain again. Tip into a bowl and toss through 1 teaspoon of the oil. Lightly beat 1 egg in a bowl and then mix together with the pasta.

Heat a large nonstick frying pan, add half the remaining oil and curl the pasta into small cakes about 3 cm (1¼ inch) wide. Add about 4 of the pasta cakes to the pan and cook for 2 minutes, flattening the cakes down with the back of a spoon. Turn the cakes over and cook for a further 1 minute until golden all over. Remove from the pan and keep warm. Repeat with the remaining pasta cakes to make about 12.

Crack the remaining 3 eggs into a small frying pan. Muddle the eggs then dollop over the mascarpone and season well. Place over a low heat and cook for a couple of minutes until just beginning to set, then cook, gently stirring, for 3–5 minutes until creamy. Add the Parmesan and season well. Place 3 pasta cakes on each serving plate, spoon over a little scrambled egg and top with strips of smoked salmon. Serve sprinkled with chives.

For easy salmon carbonara, cook 400 g (13 oz) angel hair pasta as above. Meanwhile, mix 2 tablespoons mascarpone and 1 beaten egg in a bowl. Drain the pasta, reserving a little of the cooking water, and return to the pan. Stir through the egg mixture and 4 slices of smoked salmon, cut into strips, adding a little cooking water to loosen if needed. Serve with extra mascarpone dolloped on top and sprinkled with chives as above. **Total cooking time 10 minutes.**

seafood pasta with garlic mayo

Serves **4**

Total cooking time **20 minutes**

2 tablespoons **olive oil**

1 **onion**, finely chopped

3 **garlic cloves**, crushed

½ teaspoon **fennel seeds**

1 teaspoon **smoked paprika**

250 g (8 oz) **angel hair pasta**, broken into 3 cm (1 ¼ inch) lengths

400 g (13 oz) **can chopped tomatoes**

750 ml (1 ¼ pints) hot **fish stock**

150 g (5 oz) **prepared squid**, cut into rings

250 g (8 oz) **mussels**, debearded and cleaned

100 g (3½ oz) **raw peeled prawns**

5 tablespoons **mayonnaise**

salt and **pepper**

handful of chopped **parsley**, to garnish

Heat the oil in a large frying pan. Add the onion and cook for 5 minutes until soft, then add 2 of the garlic cloves and cook for a further 1 minute. Stir in the fennel seeds, paprika and pasta and stir for 1 minute until coated.

Pour in the tomatoes and stock, season and bring to the boil. Simmer for 10 minutes, then add the squid, mussels and prawns and cook for 3–5 minutes until the seafood is cooked through, discarding any mussels that don't open.

Meanwhile, mix the mayonnaise with the remaining garlic. Serve with the pasta, which has been scattered with the parsley.

For quick spicy seafood spaghetti, cook 500 g (1 lb) fresh spaghetti according to packet instructions, then drain and return to the saucepan. Add 1 small crushed garlic clove, 2 chopped tomatoes, 1 chopped chilli, 125 g (4 oz) cooked peeled prawns, 125 g (4 oz) cooked shelled mussels and 2 tablespoons olive oil. Squeeze over a little lemon juice, add a handful of chopped parsley, season to taste, then toss together and serve. **Total cooking time 10 minutes.**

seared steak & goulash tagliarelle

Serves **4**

Total cooking time **30 minutes**

2 tablespoons **olive oil**

1 **onion**, thinly sliced

1 **red pepper**, cored,
   deseeded and chopped

1 tablespoon **smoked paprika**

400 g (13 oz) **can chopped
   tomatoes**

2 **thick beef steaks**

325 g (11 oz) **tagliarelle**

50 ml (2 fl oz) **soured cream**

salt and **pepper**

Heat 1 tablespoon of the oil in a large saucepan, add the onion and cook gently for a couple of minutes until softened. Stir in the red pepper and cook for a further 5 minutes until softened. Add the paprika and tomatoes, then season well. Bring to the boil, reduce the heat and simmer for 15 minutes.

Meanwhile, heat a griddle pan until smoking hot. Rub the remaining oil over the beef steaks and season well. Add to the pan and cook for 2–4 minutes on each side, depending on how you like your meat cooked. Leave to rest for 5 minutes and cut into bite-sized pieces.

Cook the pasta in a large saucepan of salted boiling water according to packet instructions until al dente. Drain, reserving a little of the cooking water, and return to the pan.

Stir the chopped steak and half of the soured cream into the tomato sauce, then mix into the pasta, adding a little cooking water to loosen if needed. Pile the pasta on to serving plates and dollop over the remaining cream.

For quick stir-fried beef & red pepper tagliarelle,
heat a little olive oil in a wok or large frying pan, add 1 chopped garlic clove and 300 g (10 oz) stir-fry beef strips and stir-fry for a minute or two, then add a pinch of dried chilli flakes, 125 g (4 oz) halved cherry tomatoes and 1 drained, chopped roast red pepper from a jar. Add a splash of water and cook over a high heat until cooked through. Meanwhile, cook and drain the tagliarelle as above. Toss through the beef mixture. Top with natural yogurt. **Total cooking time 10 minutes.**

index

acknowledgements

Commissioning editor: Eleanor Maxfield
Designer: Tracy Killick
Editor: Pauline Bache
Assistant production manager: Caroline Alberti

Photography: Octopus Publishing Group Stephen Conroy
13, 59, 63, 120-121, 178-179; Will Heap 1, 6, 7 left, 7 right,
8, 55, 73, 93, 99, 115, 119, 127, 129, 133, 143, 161, 175,
193, 195; Lis Parsons 10-11, 70-71, 79, 89, 95, 101, 109,
131, 141, 145, 155, 159, 163, 165, 169, 177, 189, 203,
217; William Reavell 21, 23, 27, 39, 45, 47, 53, 57, 61, 67;
Craig Robertson 4-5, 9, 15, 17, 25, 31, 33, 35, 37, 41, 43, 51,
69, 75, 77, 81, 83, 85, 87, 91, 97, 105, 107, 111, 113, 123,
125, 135, 137, 139, 147, 149, 153, 157, 167, 171, 173, 181,
185, 187, 197, 199, 201, 205, 207, 209, 211, 213, 215, 223,
225, 227, 229, 233; William Shaw 2-3, 19, 29, 49, 65, 103,
117, 151, 183, 191, 219, 221, 231.